IVORY WHITE

Isle Of Man Travel Guide

Contents

1

Introduction

Unveiling the Isle of Man: A Celtic Treasure Trove

The Isle of Man, emerging from the depths of the Irish Sea, attracts visitors with its fascinating attractiveness, a dazzling combination of Celtic heritage, rough scenery, and a rich cultural tapestry. This self-governing British Crown dependent located between England, Ireland, and Scotland has enchanted travelers for generations.

A Historical Tapestry

The history of the Isle of Man is as compelling as its landscape, dating back to the mysterious Celts who originally settled on the island some 6,500 years ago. The island has seen the rise and fall of kingdoms, the ebb and flow of invaders, and the lasting spirit of its Manx people throughout millennia.

The ancient burial mounds, the evocative Manx language, and the traditional Tynwald, the world's oldest continually running parliament, all bear the impression of Celtic influences. Vikings, Norsemen, and Normans all left an unmistakable stamp on the island, erecting imposing castles and molding its cultural environment, adding layers of complexity and intrigue to its historical tale.

A Natural Wonders Symphony

The landscapes of the Isle of Man are a symphony of natural beauty, with jagged coasts meeting undulating hills and green glens. For those seeking an energizing commune with nature, the island's mountainous center, topped by Snaefell, its highest peak, provides spectacular panoramas and exciting hiking paths.

Dramatic cliffs drop into the Irish Sea along the shoreline, their aged faces telling tales of time and perseverance. Secluded coves and sandy beaches urge travelers to repose in the serene embrace of the ocean's rhythm. The island's rich fauna, which includes puffins, seals, and basking sharks, adds another degree of enchantment to its natural beauty, providing an opportunity for wildlife aficionados to study and enjoy the island's delicate equilibrium.

A Multicultural Mosaic

The cultural fabric of the Isle of Man is a dynamic combination of Celtic customs, Manx folklore, and modern influences, resulting in a distinct and engaging cultural identity. The Manx language, a Celtic dialect with Norse and Gaelic roots, preserves historical idioms and practices that continue to form the island's cultural identity.

Traditional Manx music fills the air at spirited ceilidhs (traditional music gatherings), where residents and visitors alike join together to celebrate the island's musical history. Through their passionate performances, Manx dance troupes exhibit the island's lively past, captivating spectators with precise footwork and bright costumes.

A Paradise for Adventure Seekers

Adrenaline junkies and outdoor enthusiasts will be in heaven on the Isle of Man, as the island's diverse landscape provides a multitude of adrenaline activities to suit a wide spectrum of adventurous spirits. The diverse geography of the island gives a plethora of opportunities to challenge personal boundaries and enjoy the excitement of outdoor hobbies, from hiking and climbing to cycling and kayaking.

The Isle of Man TT, a classic motorcycle race that has enthralled racing fans for over a century, is a must-see for any adrenaline junkie. The twisting roads and hazardous twists of the 37-mile Snaefell Mountain Course test riders' ability and stamina, creating a display of speed, agility, and courage that has become associated with the island itself.

A Delightful Culinary Experience

The culinary scene on the Isle of Man is a delectable blend of fresh, local vegetables and traditional Manx cooking, delivering a symphony of flavors to tickle the taste senses. Fresh seafood, gathered daily by local fishermen, is featured prominently on menus, highlighting the wealth of the Irish Sea as well as the island's culinary expertise. Manx kippers, smoked Manx Queenie scallops, and hearty Manx stew are just a few of the island's culinary highlights, with each dish a monument to the island's rich culinary legacy and the chefs' devotion.

A Destination for Everyone

The Isle of Man guarantees an amazing experience whether you want historical immersion, cultural inquiry, or outdoor excursions. Its enthralling combination of Celtic charm, natural beauty, and rich tradition makes it a destination for people of all ages and interests. The Isle of Man has something for everyone, from history lovers to nature enthusiasts, adventure seekers to cultural connoisseurs, providing an engaging and unforgettable experience.

A Guide to Seamless Transportation on the Isle of Man

Travel to the enthralling Isle of Man, where a flawless transportation network awaits to whisk you away to its hidden jewels and renowned sites. With its well-connected infrastructure and numerous transit choices, exploring the island is a snap, from the busy city of Douglas to the charming villages that dot the coastline.

Van Nin's Bus for Exploration

The island's public bus service, Bus Vannin, operates a vast network of routes connecting major towns, villages, and tourist areas. Bus Vannin is a fantastic alternative for visiting the island at your leisure, with regular departures and low costs. The buses are contemporary and luxurious, with accessibility features and real-time journey information.

The Douglas Bay Horse Tramway Transports You Back in Time

Take a ride on the renowned Douglas Bay Horse Tramway, the world's oldest continually functioning electric horse-drawn tramway, for a nostalgic experience. Since 1897, the lovely historical tram known as the "Snaefell" has been hauling passengers along the Douglas Bay promenade.

The Railways of the Isle of Man: A Historical Journey

Ride the Isle of Man trains, a network of heritage trains

that provide a unique perspective of the Manx landscape, to immerse yourself in the island's rich history. The Isle of Man Steam Railway, founded in 1873, offers a lovely trip around the southern coast, while the Manx Electric Railway, founded in 1894, offers a delightful excursion along the Douglas Bay shore.

Ascend the Snaefell Mountain Railway to the Summit

Take the Snaefell Mountain Railway to the summit of Snaefell, the island's highest peak, for stunning vistas and a taste of adventure. This ancient electric mountain train, which opened in 1904, rises almost 600 meters to the peak, providing panoramic views of the island and its surroundings.

Convenience at Your Fingertips: Taxi Services

Taxi services are widely accessible around the island for individuals wanting a more customized and convenient means of transportation. Licensed taxi drivers provide dependable and fast transportation to your selected locations, guaranteeing a stress-free travel experience.

Car Rentals: Travel at Your Own Pace

Car rental services are commonly accessible for individuals who want to tour the island at their speed. You may simply hire a car that meets your needs and start on a road trip throughout the island with a range of rental alternatives to pick from.

Cycling and Walking: Discovering Hidden Treasures

The Isle of Man is a biker and walker's paradise, with various pathways and routes winding through the island's different landscapes. Exploring the island on foot or bike, from seaside routes to wooded trails, gives a unique and immersive experience.

Transportation Accessibility: Providing an All-Inclusive Experience

The Isle of Man is dedicated to making accessible transportation available to all tourists. Accessible features are featured on Bus Vannin buses, and dedicated accessible parking spots are available at important attractions and public buildings.

Transportation Hints for a Trouble-Free Trip

Here are some helpful hints for a seamless and happy travel experience:

Learn about bus routes and schedules by using the Bus Vannin website or app.

Purchase a bus pass for reduced costs and unrestricted travel within certain zones.

For real-time travel information and ticket purchasing, download the Isle of Man Railways app.

For peak-season travel, consider purchasing tickets in advance.

Keep the tram timetable in mind and plan your travel appropriately.

Respect other passengers and adhere to the tram's laws and regulations.

Enjoy the picturesque drive and take in the beauty of the island.

The Isle of Man is a location that is easily visited and enjoyed by anyone, thanks to its well-connected transportation network and numerous possibilities. Whether you prefer the ease of public transit, the nostalgia of historic trains, or the independence of self-guided exploration, the island's transportation system will link you to the island's intriguing attractions and hidden jewels. Set out on your Isle of Man quest to find the treasures that await.

Accommodations for Every Traveler: Your Isle of Man Home Away from Home

The Isle of Man, a charming island tucked in the Irish Sea, has a wide range of lodgings to suit any traveler's style and budget. The island's hospitality industry is eager to welcome you with open arms, from elegant hotels to warm bed & breakfasts, and lovely self-catering cottages to unique glamping experiences.

A Touch of Luxury in Hotels

The Isle of Man has several expensive hotels that cater to a sophisticated audience for those looking for a touch of luxury and pampering. There is a hotel to suit your taste and preferences, whether you want the grandeur of a Victorian-era facility or the slick modernism of a contemporary resort.

The Hotel Sefton: The Sefton Hotel, located on Douglas Bay's seafront, emanates elegance and sophistication. This hotel is a refuge for people looking for a luxury vacation, with its lavish décor, spacious accommodations, and great service.

Hotel The Empress: The Empress Hotel is a landmark in Douglas, steeped in history and elegance. This hotel, which was formerly visited by kings and dignitaries, combines historic elegance with modern comforts.

The Hotel Welbeck: The Welbeck Hotel, located in the center of Douglas, provides a taste of boutique luxury. This hotel is ideal for discriminating tourists due to its trendy furnishings, customized service, and attention to detail.

A Home Away from Home: Bed and Breakfast

Bed & breakfasts on the Isle of Man provide a warm and friendly atmosphere for people looking for a more customized and private encounter. With comfortable lodgings, substantial breakfasts, and local insights from your hosts, these quaint places give a taste of Manx hospitality.

Albany House Bed and Breakfast: Albany House Bed & Breakfast is a delightful getaway located in the scenic hamlet of Peel. With its Victorian-era decor, comfy accommodations, and delectable breakfasts, this B&B is ideal for those looking for a peaceful retreat.

Creggans B&B: Creggans B&B offers a serene sanctuary in a secluded position overlooking Douglas Bay. This B&B is ideal for visitors seeking leisure and tranquillity, thanks to its kind hosts, spacious accommodations, and wonderful sea views.

Glen Mona Country Guest House: Glen Mona Country Guest House is a quiet getaway nestled among the undulating hills of Laxey. This guest home is ideal for anyone looking for a truly Manx experience, with its friendly welcome, spacious accommodation, and lovely rural views.

Self-Catering Cottages: A Base of Operations for Exploration

Self-catering cottages on the Isle of Man are ideal for individuals looking for independence and the opportunity to explore at their speed. These lovely cottages, distributed across the island's varied landscapes, offer a sense of local life as well as a comfortable base for discovering the island's hidden beauties.

Eary Mannin Cottage: Eary Mannin Cottage is a quaint and traditional refuge located in the lovely hamlet of Port Erin. With its stone walls, open fireplace, and serene surroundings, this home is ideal for anyone looking for a relaxing retreat.

The Old School House: The Old School House, located in the picturesque town of Kirk Maughold, offers a unique and historic getaway. This cottage is ideal for anyone looking for a taste of Manx tradition, with its original schoolhouse elements, pleasant accommodations, and peaceful surroundings.

Ballagyr Cottage: Nestled among Ballagyr's undulating hills, Ballagyr Cottage offers a calm and picturesque refuge. This home is ideal for anyone looking for a truly Manx experience, thanks to its spectacular views, excellent lodgings, and accessibility to nearby activities.

Glamping: A One-Of-A-Kind Outdoor Experience

The Isle of Man has a growing array of glamping lodgings for individuals looking for an adventurous and immersive experience. These one-of-a-kind retreats allow interaction with nature in comfort and luxury, delivering a taste of outdoor life amidst the island's breathtaking scenery.

The Glamping Pod: The Glamping Pod, located on a working farm in the Manx countryside, provides a unique and rustic hideaway.

2

Making Plans for Your Isle of Man Adventure:

Welcome to the Isle of Man, an amazing island set in the Irish Sea with Celtic charm, rugged vistas, and a rich cultural tapestry. Set off on an amazing tour with this thorough book, designed to help you plan your ideal Isle of Man experience.

Uncovering the Treasures of the Isle of Man: Must-See Locations

Peel Castle sits as a powerful sentinel on a rocky islet off the coast of Peel, murmuring tales of Vikings, lords, and sieges. Explore the island's towers, dungeons, and Great Keep, and immerse yourself in its fascinating past.

Laxey Wheel: Behold the engineering marvel that is the world's largest operating waterwheel, the Laxey Wheel. Witness its magnificent rotation, which was formerly used to pump water from Laxey Mines, and travel back in time to the island's industrial history.

Rushen Castle: Rushen Castle, a towering fortress that has kept vigil over the island for generations, transports you to the heart of Manx history. Explore its medieval towers, battlements, and Great Hall to learn about Manx royalty.

Immerse Yourself in Manx Traditions Through Cultural Tapestry

Manx Museum: Explore the rich past of the Isle of Man at the Manx Museum, a treasure trove of relics, exhibitions, and interactive displays. Travel back in time, from ancient settlements to Viking attacks and Victorian traditions, to obtain a better grasp of the island's distinct culture.

Cregneash Folk Village: A living museum that recreates traditional Manx life, Cregneash Folk Village transports visitors back in time. Wander among thatched huts, investigate the blacksmith's forge, and get a personal look at the island's agricultural past.

Manx National Heritage: Immerse yourself in the cultural fabric of the Isle of Man by visiting the Manx National Heritage sites and attractions. Learn about the island's rich history and culture by exploring its ancient burial sites, Viking villages, and medieval castles.

Outdoor Adventures: A Nature Lovers' Paradise

Snaefell Mountain: Climb to the top of Snaefell, the Isle of Man's tallest mountain, for stunning panoramic views. Ascend by the Snaefell Mountain Railway or a strenuous trek, and revel in the sense of accomplishment that awaits at the summit.

Ayre Valley: Discover the picturesque Ayre Valley, a refuge for nature lovers. Hike along its peaceful pathways, ride through its stunning landscapes, and explore the coast's secret coves and isolated beaches.

Manx Nature Trust: Join the Manx Wildlife Trust on a nature excursion to safeguard the island's unique biodiversity. Observe puffins and seals in their native habitats, find uncommon butterflies and wildflowers, and develop a better understanding of the island's delicate ecosystems.

Manx Delights: A Taste of Manx Cuisine

Fresh Seafood: The wealth of fresh seafood on the Isle of Man is a cornerstone of its culinary culture. Savor succulent Queenie scallops, freshly caught kippers, and rich seafood stews, all steeped with the island's maritime history.

Manx Loaghtan Lamb: Savor the distinct flavor of Manx Loaghtan lamb, a local breed renowned for its soft and tasty flesh. Try traditional meals like Manx lamb stew or a gourmet Manx lamb burger, all of which highlight the island's culinary pride.

Manx Kippers: A classic smoked herring delicacy, Manx Kippers will take you on a gastronomic excursion. Savor its rich, salty flavor, which is commonly served with brown bread and butter, and get a taste of Manx cuisine.

Itinerary Planning: A Guide to Seamless Exploration

Douglas Bay: Immerse yourself in the colorful atmosphere of the island's capital, Douglas Bay. Stroll down the bustling promenade, checking out the stores and eateries.

Seasonality and Timing: Discovering the Best Season to Visit the Isle of Man

Traveling to the Isle of Man, a charming island tucked in the Irish Sea is a decision that will provide an amazing experience. However, understanding the complexities of seasons and timing is critical to ensuring you optimize your stay and enjoy the island's beauty in its greatest form.

Spring: A Rejuvenating Rebirth

Spring (March-May) on the Isle of Man is a time of renewal as nature awakens from its winter slumber. Daffodils, primroses, and bluebells blanket the meadows and forests, transforming the scene into a tapestry of vivid colors.

Easter Celebrations: Immerse yourself in the cultural traditions of the island during the Easter celebrations. Witness the Manx Loaghtan Sheepdog Trials, a one-of-a-kind demonstration of canine agility, or take part in the traditional Manx Easter Egg Hunt, a family-friendly activity.

Spring is a wonderful season to explore the island's different landscapes on foot or by bike, thanks to cooler temperatures and extended daylight hours. Explore stunning coastal hikes, secret routes across the countryside, or cycling through charming communities.

Summer Activities: A Vibrant Tapestry

Summer (June-August) is the prime season for the Isle of Man, with long daylight hours and pleasant temperatures. The beaches are packed with sunbathers and swimmers, and the towns and villages are alive with activity.

Isle of Man TT Races: Immerse yourself in the thrills and excitement of the world-famous Isle of Man TT Races, a classic motorcycle racing event that attracts fans from all over the world. Witness courageous motorcyclists push their motorbikes to their limits as they race down the difficult Snaefell Mountain Course.

Manx National Day: On July 5th, celebrate Manx National Day, a happy festival that recognizes the island's distinct identity and tradition. At bustling street festivals, you may see traditional Manx dance, listen to soulful Manx music, and experience the flavors of Manx food.

Outdoor Activities: Summer is a haven for outdoor enthusiasts. Hike to the summit of Snaefell, the island's highest mountain, kayak along the rough coasts, or scuba dive or snorkel to see the diverse marine life.

Autumn: A Calming Canvas with Autumnal Colors

Autumn (September to November) paints the Isle of Man in a hypnotic spectrum of seasonal hues. The leaves change to blazing red, golden yellow, and deep orange, providing a beautiful display against the island's scenery.

Manx Food and Drink Festival: In September, indulge in the gastronomic delights of the island at the Manx Food and Drink Festival. Taste local delicacies, learn about Manx artisan food, and watch live culinary demos by famous chefs.

Heritage Open Days: Immerse yourself in the rich history of the island during Heritage Open Days, which take place in September. Explore historic locations, discover hidden jewels, and learn about Manx heritage with guided tours and exhibitions.

Autumnal Walks and Cycling: Autumn provides a peaceful setting for exploring the island's scenery. Take a stroll through fall forests, ride along gorgeous paths, or have a relaxed picnic in the calm surroundings.

Winter: A Cozy Enclave of Festive Joy

The Isle of Man is transformed into a comfortable refuge throughout the winter (December-February), with festive happiness permeating the air. The cities and villages on the island are decked out in glittering lights, and traditional Christmas markets provide a taste of seasonal delicacies.

Christmas Celebrations: Get into the holiday mood this season. Visit the charming Christmas markets, eat traditional Manx Christmas cuisine, and listen to the touching Carol Concerts presented in churches and town squares.

New Year's Eve Celebrations: Ring in the New Year on the Isle of Man with amazing festivities. As you celebrate the new year, enjoy exciting celebrations, breathtaking fireworks displays, and the island's warm and inviting vibe.

Winter Treks & Wildlife Observation: Winter provides possibilities for peaceful treks along snow-covered coasts or through calm woods. Observe the different species on the island, including puffins, seals, and basking sharks, as they thrive in their native environments.

Finally, the Isle of Man provides a thrilling experience throughout the year, with each season bringing its distinct attractions. Whether you're looking for summer's dynamic energy, autumn's quiet beauty, winter's festive joy, or spring's invigorating awakening, the island's various landscapes and rich cultural tapestry offer an amazing voyage.

Packing Essentials: Getting Ready for an Unforgettable Isle of Man Experience

Waterproof Outerwear: For those unexpected showers, a lightweight waterproof jacket or raincoat is essential. To reduce overheating, choose a breathable material, especially for treks or other outdoor activities.

Comfort Layers: Bring a mix of light and warm layers, such as long-sleeved shirts, sweaters, and a fleece jacket. This allows you to modify your apparel as the weather changes.

Pack sturdy walking shoes or boots for exploring the island's different terrains, which range from rocky coastline pathways to magnificent mountain trails. For casual strolls and beach days, choose comfortable sandals or sneakers.

Accessories: Packing intelligently will guarantee a seamless and delightful experience as you begin your journey to the beautiful Isle of Man, located amidst the Irish Sea. The island's varied landscapes and weather conditions necessitate a well-prepared traveler, ensuring you're ready for whatever adventure is ahead.

Adapting to the Manx Climate Through Clothing

The weather in the Isle of Man is unpredictable, with regular showers and brief periods of sunlight. It is critical to pack adaptable apparel that can be layered and adapted to changing situations.

the cooler months, enhance your comfort and style with accessories such as a scarf, hat, and gloves. A sunhat and sunglasses are required for outdoor activities throughout the summer.

Outdoor Adventure Essentials

The Isle of Man is a haven for outdoor enthusiasts, with activities ranging from hiking and cycling to kayaking and animal watching. Packing the appropriate equipment will improve your outdoor excursions.

A lightweight daypack is crucial for taking supplies on hikes, bicycle adventures, and day getaways. To protect your goods from the weather, make sure it's comfy and water-resistant.

Water Bottle: Carry a reusable water bottle with you on your trips to stay hydrated. To keep your energy levels up, fill it up at water fountains or streams along the trip.

Snacks: Bring energy snacks to keep you going during your outdoor activities. Granola bars, almonds, and trail mix are quick and easy energy sources.

Bring a map or compass, especially if you're hiking in rural places. A GPS gadget or a smartphone navigation app might also be useful.

To be prepared for small injuries, pack a simple first aid kit containing vital materials such as bandages, disinfectant wipes, and pain medications.

Travel Essentials for a Stress-Free Journey

Pack the following essential travel goods to guarantee a pleasant and trouble-free journey:

Keep your passport, travel insurance documents, and any other important travel paperwork organized and easily accessible.

Travel adaptor: If you're visiting from outside the UK, bring a travel adaptor to charge your electrical gadgets.

Luggage Lock: Use a luggage lock to secure your things, especially while checking in your bags at airports or transit hubs.

Travel Wallet: A travel wallet organizes and secures your currencies, credit cards, and other valuables.

Travel Pillow and Blanket: Use a travel pillow and a small, lightweight blanket to improve your comfort on lengthy travels.

Getting Used to the Island's Way of Life

Pack the following goods to embrace the Manx way of life:
Reusable Shopping Bag: Carrying a reusable shopping bag can help you reduce your environmental impact. Manx retailers support eco-friendly methods and appreciate your efforts.

With a camera or smartphone, capture the island's magnificent scenery, attractive towns, and vibrant culture.

Manx Phrasebook: Learn a few key Manx words to improve your interactions with locals and immerse yourself in the culture of the island.

Considerations for Packing for Different Seasons

While the Isle of Man is gorgeous all year, packing tips differ based on the season:

Pack layers, waterproof gear, and comfortable footwear for variable weather in spring and autumn. A small umbrella or rain poncho might also come in helpful.

Summer: To enjoy the island's beaches and outdoor activities, bring sunscreen, a hat, sunglasses, and a swimsuit. For chilly evenings, a light cardigan or sweater is useful.

To fight the colder conditions, bring warm gear such as a fleece jacket, gloves, a beanie, and a scarf. Waterproof boots are required in rainy and snowy weather.

Check the weather prediction for the Isle of Man before you leave so you can pack properly. Packing properly for your Isle of Man journey will guarantee you have all you need to explore the island's different landscapes, immerse yourself in its rich culture, and create wonderful memories. Accept the island's distinct appeal and let its energy lead you on a voyage of discovery and enjoyment.

Visa and Currency Considerations: A Practical Guide

As you prepare to travel to the enthralling Isle of Man, tucked in the Irish Sea, make sure you satisfy the visa requirements and understand the local currency. This will ensure a smooth and stress-free visit. This book will provide you with the information you need to manage the practicalities of visiting this wonderful island.

Visa Prerequisites:

As part of the British Crown, the Isle of Man is subject to UK visa rules. The requirement for a visa to enter the Isle of Man is determined by your nationality and the purpose of your stay.

Visa-Free Entry: Citizens of most nations, including the United States, Canada, Australia, New Zealand, and the majority of European Union countries, are not required to get a visa to enter the Isle of Man for stays of up to 90 days.

Visas are required for citizens of some countries, including India, China, and Russia, to enter the Isle of Man. Online visa applications can be submitted via the UK Visas and Immigration website.

Extension of Stay: If you want to stay longer than 90 days, you must apply for an extension of stay through the Isle of Man Immigration Service.

Considerations for Currency:

The pound sterling (£) is the official currency of the Isle of Man. The British pound is split into 100 pence (p).

money convert: Banks, bureau de Change offices, and certain hotels will convert your foreign money for pounds sterling. ATMs are extensively distributed and accept the majority of major credit and debit cards.

Cash is still generally accepted, although credit and debit cards are now regularly utilized. Contactless payment is becoming more widespread, and you may often pay for modest items by tapping your card.

Tipping is not expected on the Isle of Man, although it is much appreciated. If you must tip, a little gratuity of 10-15% is deemed reasonable.

Tax-Free Shopping: With no VAT or sales taxes, the Isle of Man is a tax-free refuge. This makes it a desirable shopping destination, particularly for electronics, perfumes, and other high-end items.

Additional Practical Suggestions:

Language: English is the official language of the Isle of Man, while Manx Gaelic is also spoken by a tiny minority.

Roaming costs may apply if you use your mobile phone outside of the UK. It is best to get a local SIM card for cheap calls and data.

The Isle of Man has a well-developed public transportation infrastructure, which includes buses and trains. Taxis are also easily accessible.

Accommodation: The Isle of Man has a wide range of lodging alternatives, ranging from quaint bed & breakfasts to magnificent hotels. Booking ahead of time is advised, especially during the busy season.

You may ensure a smooth and pleasurable trip to the Isle of Man by understanding the visa procedures, currency conversion, and other practical issues. Explore the island's breathtaking scenery and dynamic villages, immerse yourself in its rich culture, and make amazing memories.

Health and Safety: A Safe and Enjoyable Journey

Prioritizing your health and safety as you begin on your journey to the lovely Isle of Man, hidden amidst the Irish Sea, is critical to ensuring a smooth and happy travel experience. This book will present you with important information on healthcare, safety precautions, and health suggestions as you explore the island's beautiful scenery and dynamic towns.

Healthcare:

Medical Services: The Isle of Man has a well-established healthcare system that includes hospitals, general offices, and pharmacies. Dialing 999 for ambulances, police, or the fire department will connect you to emergency services.

Comprehensive travel insurance is always advised to cover any unforeseen medical bills that may emerge during your vacation. Check that your coverage covers the costs of medical evacuation, hospitalization, and repatriation.

Prescription and over-the-counter drugs are widely available at pharmacies. If you require special drugs, bring a copy of your doctor's prescriptions.

Safety precautions:

Personal Safety: While the Isle of Man is usually regarded as a safe destination, it is always prudent to practice caution and common sense. Keep your valuables protected, avoid wandering alone at night in quiet locations, and be aware of your surroundings.

Road Safety: The Isle of Man's road network is well-maintained, and traffic drives on the left side of the road. Drive with caution, especially on tiny coastal roads, and follow local traffic regulations and speed restrictions.

Outdoor Safety: Be mindful of potential risks like cliff edges, strong currents, and uneven terrain when enjoying the island's natural beauty. Wear adequate footwear, adhere to safety precautions, and respect the natural environment.

Health Advice:

Stay Hydrated: Drink lots of water throughout your vacation to stay hydrated, especially in hot weather and when participating in outdoor activities.

Enjoy the fresh fish, local products, and traditional Manx cuisine on the island. To keep your energy levels up, eat balanced meals and snacks.

Insect Protection: Use insect repellent throughout the summer months to protect yourself from mosquitoes and ticks, which may spread illnesses.

Sun Protection: Use sunscreen with an SPF of at least 30 daily, especially on sunny days, to protect your skin from UV radiation.

Relaxation: Make time to unwind on your journey to allow your body to rejuvenate and avoid tiredness.

You may reduce dangers, increase fun, and create unique memories on your Isle of Man journey by following these health and safety precautions. With confidence and peace of mind, embrace the island's distinctive charm, immerse yourself in its rich culture, and explore its stunning scenery.

3

Exploring the Enchanting Landscape of the Isle of Man

The Isle of Man, a treasure situated in the Irish Sea, has a variety of sceneries that enchant the spirit. The island has something for everyone, from rocky coasts and rolling hills to quaint villages and dynamic towns.

Discovering the Natural Beauty of the Island:

Snaefell Mountain: At 54°16′30″N 4°34′30″W, climb to the summit of Snaefell Mountain, the island's highest peak (530 meters). Witness spectacular panoramic panoramas of the island's varied geography, from the Irish Sea to the rolling hills and valleys. Take the Snaefell Mountain Railway, a lovely Victorian steam train that provides a unique viewpoint on the ascent.

Manx National Glens: Take a trip through the Manx National Glens, a series of four beautiful valleys formed by glaciers. Hike or ride your bike along picturesque paths, swim in crystal-clear waterfalls, and find hidden jewels like Glen Maye Falls and Ballaglass Glen. Glen Mona, with its cascading waterfall and rich foliage, is an especially lovely location for a picnic meal.

Ayre Valley: Visit the lovely Ayre Valley, a refuge for nature lovers. The picturesque Ayre Coastal Path is a 25-mile route that offers spectacular views of the coastline as well as rich birds. Seals may be seen lounging on the cliffs, while dolphins can be seen playing in the waters. Alternatively, pedal through the peaceful landscape of the valley, pausing to see the historic farms and attractive towns.

2. Visiting the Island's Thriving Towns

Douglas: Immerse yourself in the dynamic capital of the island, Douglas, located at 54°09′N 4°29′W. Take a stroll along the lively Douglas Promenade, which stretches for a mile along the bay and offers panoramic views. Investigate the Victorian buildings, such as the magnificent Villa Marina and the Gaiety Theatre, which is famed for its outstanding performances. Visit the Manx Museum, a treasure mine of relics and displays that provide an in-depth look at the island's history and culture. Enjoy the town's vibrant eating scene, which includes everything from traditional Manx dishes to modern cafés and international eateries.

Peel: Peel, located at 54°13′N 4°44′W, is a lovely port town with historical beauty. Peel Castle, a strong 11th-century fortification built on a rocky islet, is worth a visit. Climb the ramparts for panoramic views of the town and port, and explore the dungeons and towers of the castle to learn about the Manx monarchy.

The Manx Marine Museum, which has intriguing exhibits on shipbuilding, fishing, and smuggling, is a great place to learn about the town's marine background. Visit the harborside eateries for delicious seafood and stroll through the picturesque alleys dotted with colorful buildings and small stores.

Ramsey: Relax in the picturesque seaside town of Ramsey, which is located at 54°18′N 4°22′W. Visit Ramsey Beach, a popular destination for sunbathers, swimmers, and surfers. Swim in the crystal-clear seas or try your hand at surfing on the waves. Investigate Victorian architecture, such as the stunning Albert Tower and the Ramsey Town Hall. Immerse yourself in the town's cultural scene by visiting the Gaiety Theatre, which is noted for its enthralling performances, or the Ramsey Courthouse Museum, which is dedicated to the town's maritime heritage.

Cregneash Folk Village:

Travel back in time to the Cregneash Folk Village, located at 54°04′N 4°35′W. With thatched houses, active farms, and artisan workshops, this living museum recreates traditional Manx life. Observe experienced artists doing traditional skills such as spinning wool, weaving fabric, and blacksmithing. Engage in chats with people costumed in historical attire to learn about the island's rural history.

Laxey Wheel: Visit the Laxey Wheel, the world's biggest functioning waterwheel, located at 54°12′N 4°35′W. This magnificent technical marvel, which was originally used to pump water from the Laxey Mines, is a testimony to the island's industrial history. Learn about the Laxey Wheel's history and operation by taking a guided tour. From the top of the wheel, take in panoramic views of the surrounding landscape.

Rushen Castle: Rushen Castle, located at 54°06′N 4°41′W, transports visitors to the heart of Manx history. Explore this imposing medieval stronghold from the 11th century. Climb the steep staircases to the battlements for breathtaking views of the landscape. Learn about the castle's grim past.

Beyond Douglas: Discovering the Isle of Man's Charming Towns and Villages

Explore the Isle of Man's hidden jewels outside the busy capital of Douglas. These tiny towns and villages, nestled in rolling hills, along gorgeous coasts, and amidst lovely valleys, provide a look into the island's rich history, vibrant culture, and spectacular natural beauty.

Port Erin (54°06′N 4°37′W): This quaint beach community has a gorgeous port, golden sands, and spectacular views of Bradda Head. Stroll down the promenade, which is lined with colorful residences and small stores, and enjoy fresh seafood at one of the harborside restaurants. Explore the ancient Ballakillingan burial mounds and Milner's Tower, which offers stunning panoramic views.

Port St Mary: Port St Mary (54°05′N 4°33′W) has a lively environment as well as a significant maritime tradition. The RNLI Lifeboat Station, the Manx Fisherman's Hut Museum, and the stately 19th-century breakwater are all worth a visit. Take a stroll along the picturesque seafront or an exciting boat ride to Calf of Man, a natural refuge filled with puffins, seals, and unusual birds.

Castletown: Visit Castletown (54°04′N 4°41′W), the former capital of the Isle of Man. Explore the majestic Castle Rushen, a historic 12th-century fortification, and stroll through the picturesque alleys dotted with typical Manx houses and stores offering local products. Visit the island's legislative building, the Old House of Keys, and immerse yourself in the town's bustling cultural scene at the Manx National Theatre.

Peel: The remnants of Peel Castle, a powerful 11th-century fortification built on a rocky islet, reveal the historical attractiveness of Peel (54°13′N 4°44′W). Climb the ramparts for spectacular views of the city and harbor. The Manx Nautical Museum teaches about the town's nautical background, while the House of Manannan, a museum dedicated to the island's Celtic heritage, reveals Viking mysteries.

Laxey: Explore the one-of-a-kind settlement of Laxey (54°12′N 4°35′W). Admire the Laxey Wheel, the world's biggest operating waterwheel, and learn about the island's industrial heritage. Explore the Glen Laxey Mines Trail and take a guided tour of the Laxey Mines Railway, pausing for a lovely lunch amidst the lush vegetation. Discover the ancient Manx ways of manufacturing woolen items at the Laxey Woollen Mills.

Kirk Michael: Enjoy the peace of Kirk Michael (54°16′N 4°38′W). Visit the historic Kirk Michael Church, one of the island's oldest churches, and tour the graveyard, which is famous for its mythology involving the Moddey Dhoo, a blackhound. The Michael Village Walk features local crafts and artwork, as well as wonderful handmade delights from the quaint cafés and tea shops.

Maughold: For hikers and birdwatchers, Maughold (54°18′N 4°31′W) is a paradise. Explore the Maughold Headland and take in the stunning views of the coastline and Snaefell, the highest peak on the Isle of Man. At the Maughold Heritage Centre, you may explore ancient burial mounds and learn about the island's Celtic history.

St John's: Visit St John's (54°14′N 4°33′W), a hidden treasure. Discover the charming hamlet hidden among rolling hills and relax in the surrounding countryside. Explore the neighboring Glen Rushen Mine Trail, as well as the 12th-century St John's Church and traditional Manx houses.

Jurby (54°23′N 4°32′W) offers a completely off-the-beaten-path experience. The Jurby Transport Museum houses a collection of historic automobiles, motorbikes, and steam engines. Birdwatchers will enjoy the Jurby Bird Observatory, which provides an opportunity to see a variety of migrating species. Take leisurely walks around the picturesque Jurby Headland and immerse yourself in the serenity and tranquillity of this hidden jewel.

Ballaugh: Ballaugh (54°17′N 4°34′W) provides a distinct combination of history and environment. Explore the Ballaugh Curraghs, a large wetland filled with wildlife and birdwatching possibilities.

Embracing the Thrill of Motorsport and Beyond on the Isle of Man TT Mountain Course

The Isle of Man TT Mountain Course, nestled among the lush vistas of the Isle of Man, is a renowned track that stirs the emotions of motorsport lovers all over the world. With its 219 curves and enthralling history, this 37.73-mile (60.72-kilometer) public road circuit has become synonymous with adrenaline-fueled racing and unbreakable human spirit.

However, the Isle of Man TT provides more than simply a spectacular race. It serves as the entryway to an island rich in history, natural beauty, and lovely settlements. Here's a more detailed guide to enjoying the TT and the island it calls home:

A Speed and Daring Legacy:
The Isle of Man TT has a long history dating back to 1907. Initially a motorcycle competition, it quickly drew great names such as Mike Hailwood, Joey Dunlop, and John McGuinness. With their brave performances and astonishing triumphs, these riders pushed the limits of speed and endurance, inscribing their names in the TT's history books.

The TT is a celebration of the human spirit, fortitude, and tenacity, not simply a race. It serves as a reminder of what can be accomplished when passion and determination come together. The Isle of Man TT delivers an experience unlike any

31

other, whether you're a seasoned racing aficionado or a beginner to the world of adrenaline-pumping battles.

The Circuit's Unflinching Test:
The Mountain Course isn't your typical racetrack. It's a twisting ribbon of asphalt that slices through the island's varied landscape, with tight curves, perilous stretches like "Verandah" and "Gorse Lea," and beautiful panoramas. This tough race demands complete concentration, excellent skill, and the ability to react to the ever-changing conditions of the open road.

While the races are exciting to watch, keep in mind that the Mountain Course is also a public road that residents use all year. Respect the riders and marshals, always observe the safety rules, and drive with caution on the island.

Seeing the Spectacle: Seeing the TT races is a memorable experience for racing aficionados. The atmosphere is tremendous, with fans lining the track in anticipation of the booming engines and the blur of motorcyclists speeding across the countryside. Grandstands give excellent viewing opportunities, while other areas provide stunning views of the course.

Apart from the racing, the festival has a lively environment with live music, food vendors, and a range of entertainment alternatives. Immerse yourself in the camaraderie and celebrate the spirit of the TT with like-minded people from all over the world.

The Manx Grand Prix and the Classic TT: The Isle of Man also holds the Manx Grand Prix and the Classic TT, in addition to the legendary TT races. These races provide exceptional possibilities for both experienced racers and enthusiasts:

Manx Grand Prix: This event, held in September, allows amateur riders to race on the Mountain Course, following in the footsteps of renowned TT champions.

Classic TT: Held in August, this event features antique bikes and racing luminaries, giving viewers an insight into the sport's past.

Whether you're a seasoned racer or a curious spectator, these events provide an opportunity to experience the Mountain Course firsthand and learn more about motorcycle racing's rich history.

Beyond the Races: The Isle of Man is more than a racing mecca. The island has plenty to offer every sort of traveler:

History buffs should visit ancient burial mounds, historical monuments like Castle Rushen, and museums such as the House of Manannan to learn more about the island's rich Celtic legacy.

Nature Addicts: Hike the lovely seaside walks, climb Snaefell Mountain, or visit the charming communities of Castletown and Peel.

Foodies should try the island's fresh seafood, and traditional Manx cuisine, and visit the local pubs and cafés.

Seekers of Adventure: Explore the coastline by kayaking, cycling, or stand-up paddleboarding, or try your hand at horseback riding or fishing.

Whatever your hobbies are, the Isle of Man offers something

for you. So, take a break from the races to explore the island's hidden treasures, quaint towns, and magnificent scenery.

Travel Advice

Planning: Because the TT attracts a significant number of tourists, book your accommodations and transport well in advance.

transit: The island's public transit system may be congested during the TT. For the greatest freedom, consider hiring a vehicle or a motorcycle.

Tickets: Grandstand and paddock access passes are available for purchase online or at the event.

Respect the riders and marshals, and always observe the safety rules.

St. Michael's Isle: A Legendary Historical Enclave

St. Michael's Isle, commonly known as Fort Island, is a mesmerizing place steeped in history and tradition. It sits majestically amidst the blue waters of Derbyhaven Bay. This rocky island, located at 54°02′53″N 4°20′34″W, provides a look into the Isle of Man's rich history and reveals amazing stories to those who go onto its beaches.

Reminiscences of a Troubled Past:

St. Michael's Isle has a history as rich as the waves that lap at its shores, dating back to the Mesolithic period. Archaeological evidence reveals early human settlements as far back as 8,000 years ago, making it one of the earliest inhabited areas on the Isle of Man.

Battles and warfare have characterized the island's checkered history. It became a battleground for control of the Isle of Man between 1250 and 1275, with fights between the troops of England, Scotland, and the Manx. These fights left a legacy of defensive buildings, including the remnants of a 12th-century church and the massive Derby Fort, which stand as mute sentinels to the island's past.

A Folklore and Myth Tapestry: In addition to its historical significance, St. Michael's Isle is woven into the fabric of Manx folklore and mythology. There are numerous legends of hidden wealth, haunting apparitions, and supernatural animals. One such tradition talks of a magical sword concealed in the depths of the island, ready to be unearthed by a deserving individual.

The "Moddey Dhoo," a spectral black dog claimed to stalk the island's hills and valleys, is also mentioned in local legend. This legendary monster is frequently connected with death and misery, and its appearance is seen as a terrible omen.

But St. Michael's Isle mythology isn't all about terror and gloom. The island is also said to be a healing and protective area. The remains of the chapel are claimed to have the ability to heal the ill, and the island itself is revered as a sacred site where spirits can rest.

A Natural Sanctuary: St. Michael's Isle is more than simply a historical place; it's also a shelter for a variety of species.

The rocky coastlines and windswept grasslands of the island provide habitat for a variety of species, including oystercatchers, razorbills, and guillemots. Visitors can frequently see seals lounging on the rocks or dolphins playing in the nearby seas.

The island's rocky landscape provides a sanctuary for plant life as well. Wildflowers like thrift, sea campion, and scurvy grass provide bright colors to the scenery. The island's marine atmosphere encourages the growth of rare coastal flora such as sea pinks, samphire, and sea thrift, making it a haven for nature lovers.

Experiencing the Magic of St. Michael's Isle: St. Michael's Isle, accessible by a tiny causeway at low tide, provides a unique chance for exploration and introspection. Visitors may roam around the ruins of the medieval church and the magnificent Derby Fort, contemplating the conflicts that took place there in the past. The rocky nature of the island, as well as the spectacular views of the shoreline, create a calm backdrop for rest and reflection.

Hiking routes provide an opportunity to explore the island's various topography and animals for those seeking a more adventurous experience. Photographers may take spectacular photographs of the island's scenery and ruins, while birdwatchers can enjoy observing diverse species. Anglers can throw their lines from the coastlines in the hopes of catching mackerel, whiting, or perhaps the rare sea bass.

A Place of Peace and Inspiration: St. Michael's Isle is a must-see for anybody interested in the history, mythology, and natural beauty of the Isle of Man. St. Michael's Isle has something for everyone, whether you're an enthusiastic historian looking to uncover the island's past, a wildlife enthusiast eager to explore its unique environment, or just someone looking for a calm retreat.

Set sail for this enthralling island and allow yourself to be taken back in time by its magnificent ruins and enthralling mythology. You'll find a genuine treasure of the Isle of Man as you explore its rocky landscape and revel in its calm beauty, a place of tranquility, inspiration, and wonderful experiences.

Castletown: A Medieval Jewel in the Making

Castletown, a lovely town steeped in history and medieval romance, is nestled among the green hills and glittering coasts of the Isle of Man. This dynamic port town, located at 54°04'N 4°41'W, gives a stunning peek into the island's rich history, enticing visitors with its majestic fortress, picturesque streets, and vibrant cultural life.

Castle Rushen: A History Keeper:
Castle Rushen, which towers above Castletown's skyline, is a testimony to the island's violent past. This enormous castle, built by the Vikings in the 11th century, has witnessed centuries of wars, sieges, and royal intrigue. Its formidable walls, towering battlements, and subterranean rooms tell tales of daring escapes and valiant knights.

Discover the mysteries buried beneath the castle's strong

stone walls by exploring its labyrinthine tunnels, and ascending the twisting stairs to the ramparts for stunning views of the town and surrounding countryside. Guided tours reveal interesting details about the castle's history, while interactive displays bring history to life.

Wandering Through Small Towns:

Castletown's lovely alleys beg exploration beyond the castle gates. Stroll down cobblestone streets surrounded by color-ful residences and small stores selling local crafts and gifts. Discover secret flower-filled courtyards and enjoy the town's architectural legacy, notably the lovely 18th-century Arbory Street buildings.

Stop for a cup of coffee in a nice café, eat at a local pub, or peruse the unique stores selling handcrafted jewelry, Manx tartans, and other locally created treasures. Allow yourself to be transported back in time by immersing yourself in the town's calm pace and welcoming atmosphere.

A Cultural Center:

Castletown is not only a historical treasure but also a thriving cultural center. Visit the Manx Museum, which is situated in the former Courthouse and Gaol, to learn about the island's rich history and tradition. Learn about the amazing artifacts, archeological findings, and the distinctive Manx culture and traditions.

Head to the Gaiety Theatre, a Victorian marvel built in 1897, for a dose of performing arts. From traditional Manx folk music to modern plays and theatrical shows, enjoy a riveting performance. There are also regular movie screenings and special events in the theatre, so there is something for everyone.

Discovering Hidden Treasures:

The allure of Castletown goes beyond its historic core. Discover hidden jewels such as the Millennium Walk, a picturesque promenade with panoramic views of Castletown Bay and the surrounding countryside. Stroll along the port and take in the colorful fishing boats that bob in the sea. It is typical to see seals lounging on the rocks or dolphins playing in the water.

Explore the neighboring Rushen Abbey, the remnants of a 12th-century Cistercian abbey, for a touch of nature. Wander among the tranquil remains, imagining the life of the monks who once lived here, and soaking in the quiet environment.

A Bridge to the Island:

Castletown is an excellent starting point for exploring the different landscapes of the Isle of Man. Drive down the coast, stopping at picturesque settlements such as Port Erin and Port St Mary. Hike or ride across the Manx countryside's undulating hills and verdant valleys, or climb Snaefell Mountain, the island's highest point, for spectacular panoramic views.

Castletown provides an exceptional experience for every tourist with its rich history, vibrant culture, and magnificent surroundings. This medieval treasure has much to offer whether you're a history buff, a cultural enthusiast, or simply looking for a beautiful vacation. So take a trip back in time, explore its intriguing streets, uncover its hidden treasures, and make memories that last a lifetime.

The Quintessential Gems of the Isle of Man: Discovering the Charm Beyond Douglas

Discover the hidden beauties of the Isle of Man by venturing outside the busy metropolis of Douglas. These tiny cities and villages, nestled among rolling hills, along gorgeous coasts, and among lovely villages, provide a look into the island's rich history, vibrant culture, and spectacular natural beauty.

Erin's Port:

This charming coastal community features a gorgeous port, golden dunes, and breathtaking views of Bradda Head. Stroll down the promenade, which is lined with colorful residences and small stores, and enjoy fresh seafood at one of the harborside restaurants. Explore the ancient Ballakillingan burial mounds and Milner's Tower, which offers stunning panoramic views.

St. Mary's:

Port St Mary has a lively environment and a strong maritime history. The RNLI Lifeboat Station, the Manx Fisherman's Hut Museum, and the stately 19th-century breakwater are all worth a visit. Take a stroll along the picturesque seafront or an exciting boat ride to Calf of Man, a natural refuge filled with puffins, seals, and unusual birds.

Castletown:

Castletown, the former capital of the Isle of Man, transports you back in time. Explore the majestic Castle Rushen, a historic 12th-century fortification, and stroll through the picturesque alleys dotted with typical Manx houses and stores offering local products. Visit the island's legislative building, the Old House of Keys, and immerse yourself in the town's bustling cultural scene at the Manx National Theatre.

Peel:

Peel Castle, a magnificent 11th-century fortification built on a rocky islet, reveals its historical charm. Climb the ramparts for spectacular views of the city and harbor. The Manx Nautical Museum teaches about the town's nautical background, while the House of Manannan, a museum dedicated to the island's Celtic heritage, reveals Viking mysteries.

Laxey:

Laxey is a one-of-a-kind community. Admire the Laxey Wheel, the world's biggest operating waterwheel, and learn about the island's industrial heritage. Explore the Glen Laxey Mines Trail and take a guided tour of the Laxey Mines Railway, pausing for a lovely lunch amidst the lush vegetation. Discover the ancient Manx ways of manufacturing woolen items at the Laxey Woollen Mills.

Michael Kirk:

Accept Kirk Michael's tranquillity. Visit the historic Kirk Michael Church, one of the island's oldest churches, and tour the graveyard, which is famous for its mythology involving the Moddey Dhoo, a blackhound. The Michael Village Walk features local crafts and artwork, as well as wonderful handmade delights from the quaint cafés and tea shops.

Maughold:

Maughold is a paradise for trekkers and birdwatchers. Explore the Maughold Headland and take in the stunning views of the coastline and Snaefell, the highest peak on the Isle of Man. At the Maughold Heritage Centre, you may explore ancient burial mounds and learn about the island's Celtic history.

Saint John's:

Step into St John's secret jewel. Discover the charming hamlet hidden among rolling hills and relax in the surrounding countryside. Explore the neighboring Glen Rushen Mine Trail, as well as the 12th-century St John's Church and traditional Manx houses.

Jurby:

Explore Jurby for an off-the-beaten-path adventure. The Jurby Transport Museum houses a collection of historic automobiles, motorbikes, and steam engines. Birdwatchers will enjoy the Jurby Bird Observatory, which provides an opportunity to see a variety of migrating species. Take leisurely walks around the picturesque Jurby Headland and immerse yourself in the serenity and tranquillity of this hidden jewel.

Ballaugh:

Ballaugh provides a distinct combination of history and environment. Explore the Ballaugh Curraghs, a large wetland filled with birds and providing chances for birdwatchers. Visit the old Ballaugh Cross and St Mary's Church, both of which are rich in history. Hike around Glen Mooar, taking in the flowing waterfalls and stunning surroundings.

Conclusion

Beyond its main city, the Isle of Man provides an unforgettable experience. Discover the charming villages, each with its distinct charm and fascinating history. Immerse yourself in the rich culture, magnificent scenery, and unique animals of the island. Whether you're a history buff, a nature lover, or just looking for a quiet getaway, the Isle of Man's hidden jewels provide something for everyone.

Port Erin: Where Seascapes and Charm Meet

Port Erin (54°06′N 4°37′W), a charming beach hamlet in the Isle of Man, is nestled among rolling hills and overlooking the beautiful waters of the Irish Sea. This lovely refuge provides a symphony of experiences, where spectacular natural beauty blends with rich history, vibrant culture, and a wealth of activities, calling visitors to experience its enchantment.

A Serene and Exciting Seascape:
The heart of Port Erin beats to the pulse of the sea. Its golden dunes, which run along the gorgeous coastline, are the ideal backdrop for creating memories. Build sandcastles with your children, walk down the beach with warm sand between your toes, or let the soothing waves wash away your cares. For the more daring, kayak across the turquoise seas, enjoy the soft spray of the sea on your face, or explore the secret coves and rock pools filled with marine life.

The harbor changes into a serene landscape as the sun sets below the horizon, filling the sky with a kaleidoscope of hues. Fishing boats bob softly on the top of the lake, their brilliant lights reflecting on the surface, creating a postcard-perfect scene. The calm chirping of crickets and the distant call of gulls permeate the air, lulling you into a state of utter rest.

A Trip Through Time:

Aside from the beach, Port Erin has a rich history that may be found in its streets and landmarks. Climb Bradda Hill to see the majestic Milner's Tower, which offers panoramic views of the hamlet and sea. This 19th-century tower functioned as a critical navigational tool for seafarers, leading them safely over dangerous waters.

Dive into the depths of time at the Ballakillingan burial mounds, which date back over 4,000 years. These fascinating mounds, veiled in whispers of ancient customs and rites, provide a peek into the lives and beliefs of the island's early occupants, pique your interest, and invite thought.

A Colorful Palette of Artistic and Culinary Delights:

The allure of Port Erin extends beyond its natural beauty and historic monuments. The community is a thriving canvas of art and culture just waiting to be discovered. Explore the galleries displaying the work of local artists, each piece reflecting the island's distinct past and breathtaking scenery. Allow the vivid colors and complex brushstrokes to take you to another world.

Attend a show at the Erin Arts Centre, where music, dance, and drama are brought to life. The lovely sounds of local musicians fill the air, as do the impassioned movements of brilliant dancers and the mesmerizing words of performers bringing stories to life. Witness the village's creative essence bloom before your eyes.

No trip to Port Erin is complete without sampling the local

cuisine. Savor fresh seafood at a harborside restaurant, where the saline air complements the perfectly cooked cuisine. Take a bite out of a fresh-picked oyster, or relish a locally caught lobster, its exquisite flavor melting in your lips.

Try traditional Manx delicacies like Kippers (smoked herring) and Queenies (flatfish), which are one-of-a-kind meals that capture the essence of the island's culinary heritage. Alternatively, a substantial pub lunch containing local meats and vegetables complemented by a pint of Manx ale is the ideal way to round off an exciting day.

Every Soul's Adventure:

Port Erin is a doorway to a world of outdoor experiences. Hike the picturesque cliff trails that lead to quiet coves and spectacular views of the coastline. Feel the wind in your hair and the sun on your face as you stroll along the rough roads, immersing yourself in the natural landscape's raw beauty.

Explore the Glen Chass's secret waterfalls and beautiful woods, a refuge of solitude and tranquillity. As you walk through the old woods, take in the fresh air and let the sound of falling water calm your spirit. Cycling enthusiasts will find several routes throughout the area, ranging from calm beach trails to demanding climbs through the undulating hills, to suit all levels of skill.

Everyone's Haven:

Port Erin's allure stems from its capacity to appeal to a wide range of interests and preferences. This village has something for everyone, whether you're a family looking for a quiet beach trip, a history buff ready to study the past, a gourmand looking for culinary pleasures, or an adventurer looking for thrills in nature.

Port Erin delivers a wonderful getaway for everyone with its welcoming environment, magnificent surroundings, and wealth of experiences. So pack your luggage, grab your camera, and set out for this enthralling beach community. Allow the salty air to caress your skin, the sound of the waves to soothe you to sleep, and the dynamic energy of Port Erin to leave you with memories to last a lifetime.

A Cultural Enrichment Journey: Uncovering the Southwest Coast's Artistic Spirit

The allure of the southwest coast extends beyond its natural beauty and historical complexity. This enthralling location also has a thriving cultural scene, with a wide spectrum of artistic expressions to enliven your experience.

A Traditional and Contemporary Art Tapestry:

The southwest coast is a treasure trove for art fans to discover. Visit the Erin Arts Centre in Port Erin, a hub of artistic expression that showcases the work of local artists. Explore exhibitions of paintings, sculptures, and ceramics, each expressing the island's distinct traditions and viewpoints.

Continue to Castletown, where the Manx National Art Gallery has a permanent collection of Manx and foreign art. Discover paintings by well-known Manx painters such as Archibald Knox and Claude Flight, as well as works by renowned European masters.

Explore the galleries and studios dispersed across the region for an insight into modern art. Engage in dialogue with local artists, learn about their creative processes, and uncover hidden treasures that embody the character of the southwest coast.

A Musical and Theatrical Celebration:

The artistic vitality of the southwest coast extends beyond visual arts, vibrantly rebounding through music and theater. Attend a performance at Castletown's Gaiety Theatre, a Victorian masterpiece that has entertained great performers and musicians for more than a century. Immerse yourself in the enchantment of theater, from enthralling plays and musicals to sensory-stimulating modern dance events.

Visit the Manx Museum and Library to get a sample of the island's musical legacy. Discover the island's rich musical history by exploring its huge collection of traditional Manx instruments and texts.

Keep an ear out for the sounds of local musicians performing in taverns and cafés as you explore. Immerse yourself in Manx folk music's rhythmic rhythms or beat your feet to the bright sounds of modern bands and vocalists.

A Tour of Craft and Culinary Delights:

The southwest coast's cultural tapestry is strengthened further by its commitment to traditional crafts and culinary traditions. Discover workshops where experienced artists create beautiful Manx wool, wood, and ceramic sculptures. Examine their time-honored skills and enjoy the one-of-a-kind master-pieces that result from their enthusiasm.

Browse through a selection of locally created souvenirs and gifts in lovely village stores and marketplaces, each steeped with the character of the island. Find the ideal keepsake to memorial-ize your vacation, from Manx tartans and hand-knitted woolen clothes to elaborate jewelry and colorful pottery.

No cultural excursion is complete without sampling the local cuisine. Savor the taste of the sea in every bite of fresh seafood at harborside eateries. Traditional Manx delicacies such as kippers and Queenies, distinctive dishes that exemplify the island's gastronomic heritage, are available.

Visit eateries that showcase the expertise of local chefs for a taste of modern Manx cuisine. Enjoy creative cuisine that highlights local products and reflects the island's changing culinary scene.

A Bold Community Spirit:

The cultural richness of the southwest coast is not limited to museums and galleries; it lives and breathes in the hearts of its inhabitants. Along the way, you'll come across a kind and inviting community ready to share their tales and customs.

Interact with the inhabitants, learn about their way of life, and listen to their interesting stories about the island's history and traditions. Participate in local festivals and activities, im-mersing yourself in the dynamic atmosphere and appreciating the southwest coast's character.

A Long-Term Impression:

Every tourist is left with a lasting image of the southwest

coast's creative tapestry, which is woven with traditional and modern art forms, music, theater, crafts, and gastronomic pleasures. It is a destination where the beauty of nature meets the artistic energy of its people, resulting in a really rewarding and unique experience.

Allow the Southwest Coast to inspire you and leave an imprint on your spirit via its creative creations. Accept the island's distinct culture and take its stories and customs with you long after your vacation is complete.

Unravel the Mysteries of a Viking Settlement (54°12′N 4°44′W)

Peel, a lovely port town steeped in history and mystery, is located on the Isle of Man's west coast. Its enthralling alleyways, overshadowed by the magnificent Peel Castle, murmur tales of Vikings, wars, and interesting legends, tempt visitors to dig into its enthralling past.

An Inscribed Viking Legacy:

Peel Castle, positioned on St Patrick's Isle and linked to the mainland by a causeway, is a reminder of the island's Viking origins. Built by the daring Norsemen in the 11th century, this great fortification experienced years of power battles, raids, and sieges. Explore its complex tunnels, climb the ramparts for stunning views of the town and sea, and let your imagination run wild as you stroll through rooms previously inhabited by Vikings.

Centuries of History Revealed:

Peel's narrative, however, goes well beyond the Viking age. History unfolds layer by layer within its walls. Explore the House of Manannan, a 19th-century museum dedicated to the island's Celtic past and displaying remarkable objects from the Neolithic era to the contemporary day. Discover the Vikings' secrets in the Viking Gallery, which displays items found from the island's archeological sites, including the intriguing "Pagan Lady" tomb with its well-preserved necklace.

A Beach Town with a Charming Atmosphere:

Peel's appeal is shown outside the castle walls in its picturesque alleyways packed with colorful residences and stores. Wander around the bustling waterfront, where fishing boats gently bob on the water and eat delicious seafood at one of the harborside restaurants. The salty aroma of the sea, the calls of gulls overhead, and the cheerful laughter of children playing on the beach fill the air.

A Naturalist's Paradise:

Peel is a paradise for nature lovers. Hike the magnificent paths along the coast, past secluded coves and craggy cliffs carved by the sea's unrelenting might. Peel Headland is a nature reserve rich with seabirds, seals, and other marine life. Kayak or paddleboard through the waves for a more exhilarating experience, experiencing the refreshing spray of the water on your face.

A Folklore and Legend-Weaved Cultural Tapestry:

Peel's essence is inextricably linked to its mythology and traditions. Learn about the Moddey Dhoo, a phantom black hound supposed to wander the island, and hear whispers of the Fynoderee, fairies who inhabit the ancient burial mounds scattered over the terrain. Explore the magical realm of Celtic beliefs and customs, where history and mythology mingle to create a tapestry of enthralling stories.

A Sensational Feast:

Peel is not complete without partaking in its gastronomic pleasures. Fresh seafood meals ranging from savory fish and chips to juicy lobster and oysters are available. Enjoy traditional Manx cuisine like kippers (smoked herring) and Queenies (flatfish), which encapsulate the spirit of the island's past.

Visit one of Peel's numerous quaint pubs to get a sense of the local pub culture. Enjoy a pint of Manx ale, which is brewed on the island, and substantial meals made with fresh, local ingredients.

A Route to Adventure:

Peel is an excellent starting point for exploring the different landscapes of the Isle of Man. Take a lovely journey across the Manx countryside's undulating hills, stopping at quaint towns along the way. Hike the difficult Snaefell Mountain, the island's highest summit, for stunning panoramic views.

A Place to Remember:

Peel provides a memorable experience whether you want historical intrigue, natural beauty, or a pleasant beach vacation. It is a location where history resonates through old buildings, the sea echoes with enthralling tales, and the spirit of adventure lurks around every turn. So pack your bags, embrace Peel's mystery, and make memories to last a lifetime.

St. John's: Revealing the Rural Charm of the Isle of Man

St. John's is a charming oasis of peace and rustic beauty nestled among rolling hills and beautiful valleys in the center of the Isle of Man. This charming village, unspoiled by the hustle and bustle of larger towns, provides a look into a simpler way of life, where time appears to slow down and tranquility reigns.

A Historic and Traditional Village:

The picturesque town green, surrounded by traditional Manx homes with their colorful façade and well-maintained gardens, is the beating heart of St. John's. This central hub serves as a meeting area for both residents and tourists, cultivating a strong feeling of community and belonging. During the summer, the green comes alive with the sounds of laughing and conversation, with families eating under mature trees, children playing with abandon, and people relaxing on seats.

Reminiscences of the Past:

The majestic 12th-century St. John's Church reflects St. John's long and varied past. This architectural marvel bears witness to the island's historical and spiritual past. Stepping into its sanctified interior, which is embellished with stained glass windows and beautiful stone sculptures, is like taking a trip back in time. The murmurs of generations gone by seem to fill the air, evoking reflection and admiration for the village's lasting history.

A Nature-Lover's Paradise:

Beyond the hamlet, the surrounding landscape opens as a nature lover's paradise. The Glen Rushen Mine Trail, a compelling trail that travels past waterfalls, forested valleys, and abandoned mine shafts, provides a peek into the island's industrial history while highlighting the natural landscape's spectacular beauty. The surrounding Ballaugh Curraghs provide a calm backdrop for animal observation for a longer stroll. Visitors may interact with the island's unique biodiversity and comprehend its ecological value by visiting this large marsh, which is filled with various wildlife.

A Culinary Adventure:

St. John's caters to all travelers' discriminating palates. The famed Tynwald Inn, a historic bar rich in local character, provides a delectable dining experience. Its menu includes both traditional Manx food made from time-honored recipes and modern meals made with fresh, locally sourced ingredients. The Greens Tea Rooms, set in a quaint Manx hamlet, welcomes travelers to sample handcrafted cakes, scones, and light lunches in a pleasant and friendly ambiance.

Recreation and Rejuvenation:

St. John's is a refuge for individuals looking for rest and renewal. A variety of relaxing spa treatments are available at charming guesthouses, allowing visitors to indulge in well-deserved pampering and emerge feeling renewed and energized. Cycling, fishing, and horseback riding are among the many outdoor activities available in the hamlet. These activities provide an opportunity to immerse oneself in the natural beauty of the surroundings while also enjoying the revitalizing fresh air and the pleasure of physical action.

A Friendly and Inviting Community:

St. John's is well-known for its kind and inviting community. Friendly inhabitants are always willing to offer tales and insights about the town and the island, giving tourists a sense of connection and belonging. The annual St. John's Festival embodies the spirit of community, bringing inhabitants and visitors together in a spectacular celebration of Manx culture. Traditional music, dancing, and food fill the air, creating a joyful environment that develops camaraderie and cultural understanding.

The Isle of Man's entry point:

St. John's is an excellent starting point for exploring the Isle of Man's different scenery and attractions. The central location of the hamlet and easy access to major highways make it an ideal starting place for day journeys to the busy city of Douglas, the rocky coastline of Peel, or the famed Isle of Man TT track. This adaptability allows tourists to adjust their schedule to their interests and discover each region's distinct character at their own speed.

A Long-Term Impression:

St. John's leaves an indelible imprint on the soul. Its rustic beauty, peaceful atmosphere, and welcoming community spirit enchant tourists of all ages. St. John's provides an amazing experience whether you're looking for a quiet retreat, a historical discovery, or an intimate connection with nature. This hidden jewel on the Isle of Man provides a once-in-a-lifetime opportunity to reconnect with oneself and enjoy life's simple joys.

Come experience the enchantment of St. John's, where time stands still, nature thrives, and tranquility reigns supreme. This lovely village welcomes you with open arms, ready to offer its distinct beauty and charm, leaving you with treasured memories that will last long after your tour is over.

The Isle of Man's Untamed Beauty & Hidden Gems: The Far North Coast

The Far North Coast of the Isle of Man, which stretches from the Point of Ayre to the Mull of Galloway, is a site of dramatic contrasts and wild beauty. This wind- and wave-sculpted coastline is a paradise for explorers, animal enthusiasts, and those seeking tranquility and stunning views.

A Rug of Rugged Cliffs and Secret Coves:

Towering cliffs formed by millennia of erosion drop into the roiling North Sea, inspiring awe and grandeur. Hidden coves and isolated beaches, on the other hand, provide calm havens for rest and introspection. Explore Glen Dhoo's quiet splendor, where waterfalls tumble down moss-covered cliffs into a sheltered bay. Explore the raw appeal of the Point of Ayre, where the wind whispers secrets over the windswept terrain.

A Wildlife Sanctuary:

The Far North Coast is a sanctuary for a wide variety of species. Look out for beautiful peregrine falcons soaring high above the cliffs, seals basking on rocky outcrops, and lively dolphins frolicking in the surf. The plethora of feathery companions, including puffins, gannets, and razorbills that nest along the cliffs, will excite birdwatchers. The Isle of Man Bird Observatory, located near Point Ayre, provides guided tours as well as a wealth of information about the island's distinctive bird species.

A Historical and Legendary Journey:

The history of the Far North Coast is replete with old ruins and intriguing stories. Explore the ruins of St. Trinian's Church, built on a cliff overlooking the sea in the 12th century, and envision the lives of the monks who once lived in this distant enclave. Discover the Manx Shearwater colony in the Calf of Man, a natural refuge steeped in myths and legends, and listen to stories about shipwrecks and secret riches that haunt the island's coasts.

A Paradise for Adventure Seekers:

The Far North Coast is an outdoor enthusiast's paradise. Hike picturesque pathways that snake across rocky cliffs and undulating hills, providing stunning views at every turn. Feel the surge of excitement as you ride over difficult courses or test your abilities on spectacular mountain biking terrain. Try sea kayaking for a unique experience, paddling through crystal-clear seas, and visiting secret coves unreachable by land.

A Taste of the Region's Delights:

After a day of touring, savor the Far North Coast's gastronomic offerings. Hearty meals created with fresh, local ingredients are served in cozy taverns and lovely cafés. Enjoy the flavor of the sea with a plate of freshly caught seafood, or for a truly genuine experience, try a traditional Manx kipper. Try the Isle of Man's famed queenies (flatfish) or a slice of Manx tart, a delectable pastry stuffed with currants and raisins, for a sweet treat.

A Haven of Peace and Reflection:

Those seeking serenity will find refuge on the Far North Coast. The location provides some of the most stunning stargazing possibilities on the Isle of Man, because of its extensive expanses of untouched coastline and little light pollution. Relax on a remote beach while listening to the rhythmic pounding of waves on the coast, or simply locate a peaceful area to think and reconnect with nature.

Unforgettable Experiences in a Land:

The Far North Coast is a location where nature's force leaves an unforgettable imprint on your spirit. It's a location where history is spoken in the wind, wildlife thrives in its natural environment, and adventure awaits around every corner. The Far North Coast guarantees an amazing voyage, whether you desire an exciting getaway, a calm retreat, or a chance to see the Isle of Man's distinctive culture and traditions.

Above and Beyond the Surface:

The fascination of the Far North Coast extends beyond its spectacular vistas and animals. The sweeping farmlands interspersed with traditional Manx farms reflect the region's strong agricultural past. Participate in talks with local farmers, learn about their sustainable methods and traditions, and enjoy the benefits of their labor by purchasing fresh food from farm stands or local markets.

For those who want to go further, the Far North Coast provides a unique opportunity to study about the island's Celtic history. Explore ancient burial mounds and standing stones, evidence of a once-thriving culture on this land. Discover archaeological marvels uncovered in the region at the Manx Museum, such as the beautifully carved Ballaugh Cross and the interesting Ballaquark stone circle.

A Place for Everyone:

Visitors are welcomed with open arms on the Far North Coast, which has something for everyone. Picnics on isolated beaches, sandcastle building, and exploring the marvels of rock pools are all options for families. Photographers may photograph stunning vistas, spectacular wildlife, and enthralling sunsets. The natural world's untamed beauty and brilliant hues may provide artists with unlimited inspiration.

Ramsey's Allure: A Historic Hub on the Isle of Man's North Coast (54°18′N 4°22′W)

Ramsey, located on the Isle of Man's north coast, combines history, natural beauty, and cultural appeal. This dynamic town, known as the "Gateway to the North," provides an excellent starting point for exploring the island's numerous offers, making it an appealing destination for discriminating tourists.

A Historical Tapestry:

Ramsey's history is revealed in its cobblestone streets and Victorian architecture, each aspect whispering tales of ages gone by. Immerse yourself in the solemn atmosphere of St. Paul's Church, which dates back to the 14th century and features elaborate stained glass windows and interesting woodwork. The Grove Museum, built in a former Victorian schoolhouse, delves further into the island's rich history. Exhibits including archeological findings, traditional Manx fabrics, and Viking age relics provide a vivid picture of the island's past.

A Nature-Embraced Coastal Haven:

Ramsey's coastline setting provides a plethora of natural attractions. Stroll down the lovely promenade, taking in the fresh sea air and listening to the rhythmic smashing of the waves on the coast. Discover Mooragh Park's hidden beauty, a huge refuge rich with varied vegetation and wildlife. Explore the park's network of walking paths, which lead to hidden beaches, tranquil lakes, and fascinating geological structures like the Queen's Pier.

A thriving cultural and artistic hub:

Ramsey's dynamic cultural scene is brimming with creative energy. At the Milntown House and Gardens, a 17th-century mansion covered with beautiful paintings, sculptures, and decorative arts, you may immerse yourself in the world of Manx art. The Gaiety Theater, a Victorian masterpiece that stages a broad selection of acts throughout the year, lets you experience the enchantment of live theater. Traditional Manx music sessions in the Ramsey Town Hall, where spirited tunes fill the air, offer a sample of the island's musical history.

Adventure and exploration begin here:

Ramsey is an excellent starting point for visiting the North Isle of Man's beautiful surroundings. Travel via stunning mountain passes and attractive villages on a picturesque tour around the famed TT Mountain Course, a motorcycle racing circuit. Hike through Glen Wyllin, a secluded valley known for its gushing waterfalls, rich foliage, and peaceful ambiance. For a more difficult experience, climb Snaefell Mountain, the island's highest point, and be rewarded with magnificent views of land and sea.

Culinary Highlights & Regional Flavors:

Ramsey's culinary scene takes you on a delicious journey via Manx history and fresh, local products. Savor the catch of the day at one of the harborside restaurants, where talented chefs translate the wealth of the sea into delectable cuisine. Experience the warmth and kindness of local pubs, where substantial meals and pints of Manx ale are offered. Indulge in flavorful Manx delicacies like kippers (smoked herring) and queenies (flatfish), which highlight the island's gastronomic tradition.

A Warm Community with a Festive Spirit:

Ramsey has a warm and inviting community. Locals are always eager to share their experiences and ideas about the island, providing a welcoming environment for tourists. Immerse yourself in the year-round exciting activities and celebrations, such as the Ramsey Town Hall Christmas Market. This delightful festival, full of Christmas joy, local crafts, and delectable cuisine, embodies the heart of the community.

A Relaxation and Rejuvenation Sanctuary:

Ramsey is a retreat for individuals looking for quiet and calm. Stroll around the beautiful beaches, letting the relaxing beat of the waves wash your concerns away. Escape to Mooragh Park, where serene gardens and forest pathways allow you to commune with nature and achieve inner tranquility.

A Journey Outside of the Ordinary:

Ramsey provides a one-of-a-kind and amazing experience that goes beyond the conventional tourist attraction. It's a location where history whispers secrets behind old walls, nature reveals its amazing beauty, and culture flourishes in its people's hearts. Ramsey guarantees a stimulating vacation that makes a lasting impression, whether you desire historical research, outdoor adventure, or a taste of local charm.

So begin on an enthralling discovery of Ramsey and discover the enthralling combination of history, natural beauty, and cultural appeal that awaits you in this thriving town on the Isle of Man's north coast.

Laxey: Uncovering the Historical Wonders of the Isle of Man

Laxey, nestled in the green hills of the Isle of Man, entices visitors with a compelling mix of historical mystery, industrial legacy, and spectacular natural beauty. This quaint hamlet, famous for its distinctive Laxey Wheel, has a particular position in the heart of the island, providing tourists with an insight into the island's rich mining history and attracting visitors with its stunning scenery and welcoming community spirit.

The Mighty Laxey Wheel: A Legacy Engraved in Steel

Lady Isabella, the renowned Laxey Wheel, unquestionably ranks as Laxey's finest gem. This magnificent edifice, erected in 1854 and regarded as the world's largest operating waterwheel, is a testimony to Victorian mechanical skill. Visitors are amazed by the wheel's sheer size and precise craftsmanship, which stands 72 feet tall and has a diameter of 72 feet. The image of the wheel in action, propelled by the raging waters of the Laxey River, is extremely enthralling.

A Glimpse of the Past: Exploring Laxey's Mining History:

Laxey's history is inextricably linked to its mining heritage. The Laxey Mining Museum, situated in the former captain's office, provides an intriguing look into the life of miners and the difficulties they encounter. Explore displays including mining equipment, tools, and antiques, each of which tells a narrative about the village's industrial background. Descend into the Earth's depths via the intriguing Laxey Mine Railway, where a ride through the tunnels and shafts shows the hidden world of the miners and the mysteries they uncover.

A Visit to Nature's Playground:

The natural beauty of Laxey is a welcome counterpoint to its industrial surroundings. Glen Roy Nature Reserve, a refuge for various flora and animals, provides a peaceful haven. Hike along the woodland trails, gaze at the flowing waterfalls, and soak in the peace. Explore the Laxey Mines Trail for a more adventurous experience, a hard hike that leads to spectacular vistas and abandoned mine shafts, providing a look into the village's past.

A Cultural and Artistic Mecca:

The artistic energy of Laxey pervades its galleries and workshops. Visit the Laxey Arts Centre to see the work of local artists, where vivid paintings, sculptures, and ceramics exhibit the island's creative flair. Interact with the artists, learn about their inspiration, and discover the ideal souvenir to remember your visit. At the annual Laxey Festival, a colorful celebration of the island's rich cultural history, immerse yourself in the world of Manx music and dance.

A Gastronomic Adventure:

Laxey's food culture caters to all tourists' tastes. Try fresh seafood at harborside eateries, where the flavor of the sea can be tasted in every meal. Traditional Manx cooking may be found in snug pubs, where hearty meals are served alongside pints of local ale. For a taste of real Manx cuisine, try kippers (smoked herring) or queenies (flatfish), both of which are flavorful meals.

Discovering the Isle of Man:

Laxey is an excellent starting point for exploring the different landscapes of the Isle of Man. Begin your journey up the Snaefell Mountain Road, stopping at quaint communities and spectacular overlooks along the route. Try cycling or mountain biking on the tough paths that meander through the hills and valleys for a more exhilarating experience.

A Neighborhood That Welcomes You:

The pleasant community of Laxey will make you feel right at home. Locals are always eager to share their experiences and views about the town and their island, resulting in a genuine and welcoming atmosphere. Engage in talks with shops, pub owners, and fellow tourists to learn about Laxey's genuine essence via its people.

Laxey is a place for leisure and rejuvenation, in addition to its historical significance and cultural attractions. Stroll along the scenic Laxey Promenade, taking in the fresh sea air and taking in the panoramic views. Allow the calming sound of the waves to wash away your troubles as you relax on the sandy beaches.

A Place of Indelible Memories:

Laxey provides an exceptional experience that extends beyond tourism. It's a location where history comes to life, nature thrives, and a welcoming community awaits you. Come experience Laxey's enchantment, uncover its hidden jewels, and make memories to last a lifetime.

Mount Snaefell: Conquering the Rooftop of the Isle of Man at 621 Meters (54°14'N 4°43'W)

Mount Snaefell, at 621 meters (2,037 feet), is the highest point in the Isle of Man. This spectacular mountain, cloaked in mist and folklore, calls out to daring individuals to embark on a difficult but rewarding climb to its peak. Prepare to be captured by stunning views, energizing breezes, and a sense of achievement that will last long after you have descended.

A Manx Historical Landmark and Symbol of Identity:

Mount Snaefell has a long history, as evidenced by the ancient burial mounds and cairns that dot the area. The name of the mountain, derived from the Old Norse words for "snow" and "mountain," testifies to its enduring presence and the reverence it has commanded for millennia. Snaefell represents resilience, fortitude, and a link to the Manx people's natural history.

A Diverse Landscape Awaits Discovery:

The trek to the peak provides an enthralling look at the Isle of Man's varied landscapes. Nature unfolds in a captivating tapestry, from the lush green valleys and rolling hills at the mountain's base to the rocky landscape and windswept plateaus on the top. Along the route, you'll see flowing waterfalls, secret tarns, and a variety of flora and animals, all of which add to the mountain's allure.

A Body and Mind Test:

There are various paths to the peak, each with its own set of challenges. The Snaefell Mountain Railway, the most popular route, offers a picturesque trip through the slope, culminating in a stunning perspective from the top station. Hiking routes wind their way up the slope, allowing a chance to fight the elements and challenge your physical stamina for those looking for a more challenging trip.

A Visual Paradise for the Senses:

The rewards for reaching the peak are simply spectacular. Panoramic views of the Isle of Man reveal undulating hills, lovely settlements, and the great expanse of the Irish Sea on a clear day. The wind tells stories about the island's history and conveys the aroma of the sea, producing a wonderfully energizing and unique experience.

A Mythical and Legendary Mountain:

For generations, Mount Snaefell has served as an inspiration for Manx mythology and stories. Fairies and legendary creatures are claimed to inhabit the mountain, and the peak itself is said to be a site of enormous power. The mountain's history and stories provide an added dimension of mystique and mystery to those who trek to the summit. A Wildlife Sanctuary:

Mount Snaefell is a sanctuary for a wide variety of species. Red grouse and mountain hares may be seen scurrying over the slopes, while peregrine falcons fly across the skies. The mountain's diverse ecosystems also sustain several types of wildflowers and plants, contributing to the landscape's natural beauty.

7. A Doorway to More Adventures:

Mount Snaefell is a starting point for further exploration of the Isle of Man. You can plan your next trip from the peak, whether it's seeing picturesque villages, visiting historical monuments, or discovering secret coves along the coast. The island has everything to offer every sort of tourist.

A Self-Discovery Journey:

Conquering Mount Snaefell is a voyage of self-discovery and personal success, not merely a physical struggle. The mountain's commanding presence evokes awe and humility, reminding you of your power and resilience. The summit experience is a wonderful one that will leave you feeling energized and powerful.

After the Summit:

Mount Snaefell is more than simply a tourist attraction; it represents the soul of the Isle of Man. It's a location where history and nature collide, old stories whisper in the breeze, and the rewards of perseverance are stunning. So put on your hiking boots, accept the challenge, and set off on an incredible trek to the rooftop of the Isle of Man.

4

Unleashing the Enigmatic Spirit of the Isle of Man: A Guide to Diverse Activities and Adventures

Beyond the Observations:

The compelling character of the Isle of Man extends beyond its spectacular activities and historical treasures. It may be found in its people's warm and friendly character, who are always happy to share their tales and customs with tourists. It is obvious in the colorful festivals and events that commemorate the island's heritage, from the electric atmosphere of the TT Festival to the delightful culinary pleasures of the Isle of Man Food and Drink Festival.

Immersions in Culture: Embracing Manx Traditions:

Immerse yourself in Manx culture's unique tapestry. Visit local craft workshops and studios where experienced artists produce one-of-a-kind objects inspired by the island's history. Discover the historical legacy of the Manx Gaelic language and see how it is being revived in schools and communities. Attend a traditional Manx music performance and get swept away by the vivid songs and enticing rhythms.

A Celestial Spectacle: Stargazing

Unravel the wonders of the cosmos beneath the beautiful night sky of the Isle of Man. The island, which is free of light pollution, provides excellent stargazing conditions. Escape to remote beaches or designated dark sky regions to see a stunning display of stars, planets, and constellations. This celestial display allows you to connect with nature and appreciate the immensity of the cosmos.

Relaxing Getaways: Soul Rejuvenation:

The lovely landscapes of the Isle of Man provide respite and tranquillity. Relax on gorgeous beaches, soak up the sun, and listen to the waves' relaxing beat. Relax in a quiet cottage surrounded by rolling hills and lovely villages, or indulge in exquisite spa treatments and yoga and meditation classes. The island provides a place for self-renewal and refreshment.

Family Outings: Making Memories Together:

The Isle of Man is an excellent destination for families. Explore the interactive exhibitions at the Manx Museum, take a thrilling ride on the Isle of Man Steam Railway, or feed animals at the Curraghs Wildlife Park. Build sandcastles on the beach, go on exciting scavenger hunts, or simply spend quality time together surrounded by nature's beauty to make memorable memories.

Memorable Journeys:

Every visitor to the Isle of Man will have a one-of-a-kind

and unforgettable experience. Whether you're looking for adrenaline-pumping thrills, peaceful retreats, or enlightening cultural encounters, the island has something for you. This book has given you a taste of what it has to offer, but the actual magic is in uncovering the hidden treasures and planning your unique adventure.

Pack your luggage, embrace the spirit of adventure, and set off on an enthralling exploration of the Isle of Man. Explore its stunning scenery, learn about its rich past, and enjoy the warm friendliness of its people. Allow the Isle of Man to work its charm and leave you with memories that last a lifetime.

Hiking and Walking in the Isle of Man: Scenic Trails and Coastal Escapes

Beyond the Paths:

The hiking and walking opportunities on the Isle of Man extend beyond the defined pathways. For the daring, the island has a wide network of unexplored routes and hidden places just waiting to be discovered. Off the main path, you'll find isolated coves accessible only by foot. Hike to the rough slopes of the island's tallest peaks, Snaefell and The Barrule, for breathtaking vistas of the land and sea. Explore the countryside for ancient ruins and historical monuments that tell the narrative of the island's rich past.

Mountain biking and trail running:

The unique topography of the Isle of Man provides a paradise for trail runners and mountain bikers looking for a more demanding and adrenaline-pumping experience. The difficult routes zigzag through forests, climb hills, and travel along spectacular cliff edges, making for an exciting test of stamina and ability. The Isle of Man TT track, famous for motorcycle racing, is now open to cyclists, providing a once-in-a-lifetime opportunity to put your skills to the test on this famed circuit.

Animal Encounters:

The fauna on the Isle of Man is diverse, making your journey even more rewarding. Look for majestic peregrine falcons flying over the cliffs, playful seals lounging on the rocks, and curious bunnies scurrying through the vegetation. The profusion of feathery companions, including puffins, gannets, and razorbills that nest along the coast, will excite birdwatchers. The Isle of Man Bird Observatory, located near Point Ayre, provides guided tours as well as a wealth of information about the island's distinctive bird species.

Picnics and refreshments are available.

Pack a tasty picnic lunch and enjoy a quiet break with stunning views. Many pathways provide picturesque settings ideal for relishing your lunch while surrounded by nature's grandeur. A picnic of smoked kippers, fresh bread, and cheese, complemented by a cool pint of local ale, is a classic Manx treat. Along the routes, several attractive villages and towns offer quiet cafés and bars where you can refuel and drink up the local vibe.

Sensory Encounters:

Hiking and walking on the Isle of Man is a visual and auditory experience. Breathe in the sea salt-infused fresh air, feel the sun's warmth on your skin, and listen to the waves pounding on the coast. Let the pleasant perfume of wildflowers and the earthy aroma of the forest wash away your cares as you take in the sights and sounds of nature.

Exploration for the Long Term:
The Isle of Man is dedicated to sustainable tourism and promotes safe hiking methods. Stay on approved paths, leave no trace, and minimize your damage to the ecosystem. Select eco-friendly lodging alternatives that help local businesses and encourage sustainable practices. You can help preserve the island's natural beauty for future generations to enjoy by doing so.

Hiking or walking in the Isle of Man is more than just exploring stunning landscapes; it's a trip that links you with nature, tests your physical boundaries, and leaves you with lasting memories. So put on your boots, take your bag, and go off on a voyage of self-discovery among the enthralling beauty of the Isle of Man's various routes and coastline getaways.

Cycling Around the Isle of Man: A Cyclist's Paradise

The Isle of Man is a cyclist's heaven, with its rolling hills, stunning shoreline, and attractive countryside. Whether you're a seasoned pro or just a casual cruiser, the island has a variety of cycling routes to suit all skill levels and tastes.

A System of Scenic Trails:

The Isle of Man has an extensive network of bike lanes and trails, making it simple to explore the island at your leisure. The Raadny Foillan, a 102-mile coastal walk, offers stunning vistas of the sea as well as lovely settlements along the way. The Millennium Way, a 146-mile round path, passes across varied scenery such as undulating hills, woods, and charming villages.

Climbs that are difficult and breathtaking descents:

The Isle of Man has lots of options for skilled cyclists looking for a challenge. With its steep inclines and tight curves, the Snaefell Mountain Road is a favorite among cyclists. The ascent to the peak is rewarded with breathtaking views over the island. The Beinn-y-Phott, with its hairpin curves and stunning scenery, and the Sulby Valley, with its rolling hills and lovely farmsteads, are two more difficult roads.

Villages and towns that welcome cyclists:

The Isle of Man is recognized for its welcoming people and bike-friendly villages. Many villages and towns cater to bikers, with bike rentals, repair shops, and lodging alternatives created exclusively for two-wheeled tourists. Locals will be pleased to give you directions, provide bike advice, and recommend local sites along the road.

The TT Course on the Isle of Man: A Legendary Cycling Challenge:

The Isle of Man TT track, famous for motorcycle racing, is also open to cycling. With its difficult hills, tight curves, and fast speeds, this 37.73-mile circuit gives a unique and enjoyable riding experience. While the TT route is difficult for the faint of heart, completing it is a great achievement for any rider.

Cultural Encounters Along the Way:

Cycling on the Isle of Man is more than simply a physical exercise; it's also a cultural experience. The paths lead you past ancient ruins, historic sites, and picturesque towns, each with its tale to tell. Visit local museums, artisan stores, and cafés to learn about the island's rich history and meet its welcoming inhabitants.

Cycling Festivals and Events:

Throughout the year, the Isle of Man conducts several cycling events for people of different skill levels and interests. In May, the Isle of Man International Cycling Week gathers elite riders from all around the world. The Manx Viking Cycle Challenge, a 100-mile off-road event, puts even the most seasoned riders to the test. Family-friendly rides, charity cycles, and themed cycling excursions are among the other activities.

Cycling for Sustainability:

The Isle of Man is dedicated to sustainable tourism and promotes safe riding activities. Many routes are car-free, providing bikers with a safe and pleasurable environment. Choose eco-friendly accommodations and local eateries to help the island's ecological practices.

Away from the Routes:

Cycling on the Isle of Man is not limited to specified routes. Off the main path, discover the island's hidden beauties. Explore isolated beaches, stunning ports, and secret waterfalls, each of which provides a distinct viewpoint of the island's splendor.

A Cycling Mecca for Everyone:

The Isle of Man has something for everyone, whether you want a relaxing family vacation, a tough mountain climb, or a cultural cycling experience. The island is a veritable cyclist's paradise, with its various routes, welcoming attitude, and stunning landscape. So grab your helmet, inflate your tires, and go off on a two-wheeled adventure.

A Golfer's Guide to the Isle of Man: Perfecting Your Swing on Scenic Courses

Become Immersed in Golf History:

You'll be walking on hallowed ground when you traverse the fairways of the Isle of Man's courses, where golfing greats have played. The island's strong golfing legacy is reflected in its well-kept courses, some of which date back to the late 1800s. Consider the echoes of former champions who constructed these difficult layouts, like Willie Park Jr. and Charles Alison, and let their legacy inspire your round.

Test Your Skills on Championship-Grade Greens:

Compete on championship-level courses intended to test your abilities. With its magnificent coastal location and links-style play, the Castletown Golf Links delivers a memorable golfing experience. Feel the rush of teeing off on the Peel Golf Club's clifftop holes, where stunning vistas of the Irish Sea follow every swing. Navigate the Mount Murray Golf Club's carefully placed bunkers and undulating greens, a monument to traditional course architecture.

Find Hidden Gems for All Skill Levels:

The Isle of Man is a refuge for novices and families, as well as a challenge for seasoned players. With its small layout and forgiving fairways, the Rowany Golf Course gives a soft start to the game. The Pulrose Golf Course, located near Douglas, provides a convenient and relaxing location for a leisurely round of golf. Head to the Port St Mary Golf Club for a one-of-a-kind experience, where clifftop holes and inland fairways mix to offer a diversified and entertaining golfing trip.

Accept the Golfing Community:

The Isle of Man's friendly and inviting environment extends to its golfing community. Interacting with local golfers is a wonderful experience that provides essential insights into the courses and the island's distinct golfing culture. You'll discover a helpful and encouraging network of golf aficionados whether you're looking for tips on tackling a difficult hole or simply looking for nice company.

Enjoy a Luxurious Getaway:

Luxury lodgings and pampering services can be added to your golfing experience. Choose from a wide range of hotels, resorts, and spa facilities that appeal to discriminating tourists' demands. After a hard round on the green, enjoy exquisite meals, relax in beautiful settings, and refresh your mind and body.

Discover the Hidden Treasures of the Island:

Step off the beaten path and explore the Isle of Man's hidden gems. Discover lovely communities such as Port Erin and Laxey, along with quaint shops, art galleries, and traditional pubs. Visit ancient monuments such as Castle Rushen and Peel Castle to immerse yourself in the island's rich history, or enjoy a picturesque walk along the stunning coastline.

Unforgettable Experiences Await Beyond the Fairways:

Combine your golfing vacation with other exciting activities for a unique experience. By foot or bicycle, explore the island's various landscapes, passing through rolling hills, valleys, and lovely towns. Enjoy the thrills of water activities like kayaking, paddle boarding, and diving, or go horseback riding in the countryside.

In a Golfer's Paradise, Make Lasting Memories:

The Isle of Man is a golfer's paradise, not merely a collection of championship courses. It's a location where you can test your skills on perfectly created greens, immerse yourself in the local golfing culture, and have memorable experiences surrounded by the island's stunning environment. So pack your clubs, make your tee times, and get ready for an incredible golfing adventure on the Isle of Man.

Uncovering the Isle of Man's Treasure Trove: A Fishing Adventure Guide

With its numerous fishing prospects, the Isle of Man, a gem in the Irish Sea, entices fishermen of all abilities. The island's waterways teem with a diversity of species waiting to be explored, from the towering cliffs and beautiful beaches to the peaceful inland lakes and rivers.

A Diverse Tapestry of Fishing Opportunities:

The Isle of Man has something for everyone, whether you're a seasoned angler searching for an adrenaline-pumping deep-sea experience or a beginner looking for a calm day on the beach. Choose from a tantalizing array of alternatives, including:

Sea fishing: Cast your line from the island's numerous piers, ports, and beaches in search of valued species such as cod, pollack, bass, and mackerel. Take a deep-sea fishing excursion and compete against larger species such as tope, tuna, and even sharks for a memorable experience.

Fishing from the island's stunning cliffs and rugged shoreline will put your skills and patience to the test. Target wrasse, flounder, and even lobster while admiring the stunning coastal environment.

Freshwater Fishing: Discover the calm lakes and rivers of the island, which are home to brown trout, rainbow trout, and salmon. For a pleasant experience, cast your fly rod in crystal-clear waterways or try classic bait fishing.

Coarse Fishing: Visit authorized coarse fisheries stocked with species such as carp, tench, and bream. Enjoy a tranquil day by the sea and immerse yourself in the beauty of your surroundings.

Accepting Guided Adventures:

Consider organizing a guided trip with a local expert for a flawless and instructive fishing experience. These knowledgeable captains and guides are well familiar with the greatest fishing sites, the most successful tactics, and the secrets to capturing the elusive fish. They will supply all required equipment and guarantee that you have a safe and pleasurable day on the lake.

Stunning Coastal Locations:

The Isle of Man has a beautiful coastline with a variety of fishing options. Popular spots include:

Douglas: The island's dynamic capital has a great pier fishing for cod, pollack, and mackerel. Take a walk along the promenade, cast your line, and soak in the bustling atmosphere of the town.

Peel: This picturesque coastal town gives access to deeper seas and excellent fishing for tope, skate, and even sharks. While you wait for a snack, take in the beautiful views and pure sea air.

Port Erin: This protected bay is great for novices and families. Cast your line from the beach or pier to catch wrasse, flounder, and place. After that, go through the lovely village and enjoy delectable local food.

Ramsey is well-known for its superb rock fishing. Climb down the cliffs, toss your line into the pounding waves, and catch wrasse, cod, and pollack.

Getting Around Regulations and Licenses:

Anglers in the Isle of Man must adhere to strict laws and receive the necessary licenses. For further information on laws, fishing seasons, licensing costs, and authorized fishing locations, see the Isle of Man Government website.

Beyond the Hook:

The Isle of Man has more to offer than just fishing. Visit ancient monuments such as Castle Rushen and Peel Castle to learn about the island's rich history and culture. Visit galleries and studios to immerse yourself in the local artistic scene, or enjoy a beautiful drive through the rolling hills and lovely towns.

A Sustainability Commitment:

The Isle of Man is dedicated to sustainable fishing techniques. Follow the catch-and-release guidelines for specific species, and respect the local ecology by leaving no trace. Support local businesses and buy sustainable seafood to guarantee that future generations may enjoy the island's abundant seas.

A Memorable Fishing Trip:

The Isle of Man provides a one-of-a-kind and spectacular fishing experience. The island is a haven for fishermen of all ability levels, with its various waterways, magnificent landscape, and friendly environment. So pack your fishing gear, pick your favorite location, and get ready to throw your line into the rich waters of the Isle of Man. You'll undoubtedly make unforgettable memories and collect stories that will last a lifetime.

The tone and organization of this rewritten text are more professional. I avoided abbreviations and utilized more formal language while retaining a clear and engaging approach. I've also included information regarding fishing rules and licensing, as well as underlined the need for sustainability.

Exploring the Isle of Man on Horseback: A Time and Terrain Journey
Uncovering the Island's Hidden Treasures:
On horseback, explore the Isle of Man's secret gems beyond the defined pathways. Discover old remains such as Balladoole Broogh, an Iron Age walled site, or the spooky beauty of the Curraghs Mines, a network of abandoned lead mines with a fascinating history. Ride along the rugged coastline, stopping at isolated coves such as Port Grenaugh for a refreshing dip or a picnic with spectacular views. Keep a look out for the island's rich fauna, such as red deer, pheasants, and even the majestic buzzard flying through the skies, while you explore.

Exploring Manx Traditions:
During your equestrian trip, immerse yourself in the lively Manx culture. Visit nearby farms to hear about traditional Manx sheepdog demonstrations, see the ability of experienced saddlers and blacksmiths, or visit a local festival with Manx music, dancing, and food. These excursions provide an insight into the heart of Manx culture and an opportunity to engage with the friendly people of the island.

Delights in the Kitchen:
After a day of horseback riding, savor the amazing gastro-

nomic scene on the Isle of Man. Traditional Manx pubs provide substantial meals such as kippers, queenies, and loghtan lamb. Try native cheeses like Manx cheddar and smoked cheese, or sip a refreshing pint of Manx beer made from island-grown barley. Try the Isle of Man's national dish, "Spiced Beef," a slow-cooked delicacy with a rich and savory heritage, for a genuinely unique experience.

Alternatives for lodging:

The Isle of Man has a variety of lodging alternatives to suit your requirements and budget. Choose from quaint bed & breakfasts, comfortable cottages, and opulent hotels. Many businesses specialize particularly in equestrians, providing stables, paddocks, and other amenities for your horse's welfare. You'll find the ideal spot to unwind and recharge after your equine excursions, whether you're looking for a rustic hideaway or a luxurious retreat.

Away from the Saddle:

While horseback riding is a must-do on any Isle of Man itinerary, additional activities should be included for a well-rounded experience. Hike or cycle along gorgeous paths, explore the island's attractive villages and towns or pay a visit to historical sites such as Peel Castle and Castle Rushen. Take a boat ride around the Calf of Man, a natural paradise and home to a unique puffin colony. Whatever your hobbies are, the Isle of Man has limitless opportunities for a wonderful trip.

A Long-Term Strategy:

The Isle of Man is dedicated to sustainable tourism and promotes safe equestrian riding techniques. Choose stables that put animal welfare first and implement ecologically responsible procedures. Stay on approved pathways and leave no evidence of your travel to protect the island's natural ecology. You may help maintain the island's beauty for future generations to enjoy by making mindful decisions.

A Journey for Everyone:

Horseback riding on the Isle of Man is suitable for people of all ages and ability levels. Riders with prior experience can go on arduous expeditions to discover the island's different landscapes. Beginners can learn to ride at approved riding schools and stables, where they can acquire confidence in a secure and friendly atmosphere and enjoy easy rides in scenic landscapes. Families may enjoy pony rides and guided excursions designed specifically for youngsters while having unforgettable experiences together.

A Timeless Getaway:

The Isle of Man provides a getaway from the stresses of everyday life. You'll leave your concerns behind as you ride over the rolling hills, breathe in the fresh air, and feel the sun on your skin. Enjoy the peace of the countryside, uncover hidden jewels, and make memories that last a lifetime. So saddle up, embrace the spirit of adventure, and go on a timeless equestrian tour around the Isle of Man.

Uncovering the Isle of Man's Wild Treasures: A Wildlife Watching Guide

The Isle of Man, with its different landscapes and natural

beauty, is a wildlife paradise. The island provides a unique opportunity to witness a range of intriguing wildlife in their natural habitats, from majestic seagulls soaring far above the cliffs to secretive seals lounging on the rocks.

A Marine Bird Sanctuary:

The stunning coastline and outlying islands of the Isle of Man provide critical nesting habitats for a variety of seabirds. At the Calf of Man, a protected bird sanctuary, you may see hundreds of puffins nesting on the rocks. At nightfall, marvel at the beautiful flight of Manx shearwaters returning to their burrows, or watch razorbills and guillemots dive for fish in the roaring waves.

Encounters on the Coast:

The shoreline of the Isle of Man is alive with activity. Grey seals can be seen sunbathing on the rocks in Port St. Mary or the Ayres Nature Reserve. Observe bottlenose dolphins playing in the waters near Peel Harbour or Ramsey Bay. Take a boat tour to see basking sharks, the world's second-largest fish, as they glide through the plankton-rich seas for a unique experience.

Explorations in the Interior:

Explore the island's abundant terrestrial biodiversity beyond the coast. Hike through Glen Helen's woodlands, keeping an eye out for red squirrels scampering amid the trees. Listen for the sounds of elusive ravens and peregrine falcons as you walk over the heather-clad hills of the Snaefell Mountain range. Visit the Ballaugh Curraghs to see wading birds including lapwings, redshanks, and oystercatchers in their natural environment.

A Butterfly and Moth Paradise:

The Isle of Man is home to a plethora of butterflies and moths, which lend a dash of color to the island's surroundings. Look for little tortoiseshells and speckled wood butterflies flying around fields and gardens. Among the wildflowers, look for the emerald green emperor moth resting on tree trunks or the spectacular orange and black cinnabar moth.

Night's Hidden Treasures:

As the sun sets, a new world emerges on the Isle of Man. Listen for the eerie sounds of owls hunting for food in the darkness, such as the tawny owl and the barn owl. Bats flit beneath the moonlight as they feast on insects in the night sky. If you're patient and attentive, you could even see a hedgehog feeding in the bushes.

Responsible Wildlife Observation:

It is critical to respect the island's fauna. Keep a safe distance from animals and avoid interrupting their natural behavior. Choose guided excursions led by knowledgeable specialists who value ethical wildlife-watching techniques. Leave no trace and stick to approved trails and routes to reduce your environmental effects.

Aside from Sightings:

The Isle of Man provides a once-in-a-lifetime chance to study animal conservation and ecological research. Visit the Manx Wildlife Trust's visitor centers to learn about the island's unique animals and current conservation efforts. Participate in volunteer activities such as beach clean-ups and bird surveys to directly help conservation efforts.

A Discovery Journey:

Wildlife viewing on the Isle of Man is more than just looking for animals; it's an adventure. It's an opportunity to reconnect with nature, appreciate its many marvels, and develop a better knowledge of the delicate balance of our environment. So take your binoculars and camera and prepare for an incredible journey into the untamed heart of the Isle of Man.

On the Isle of Man, Embracing the Thrill of Water Sports: Surfing, Swimming, and Sailing Adventures

With its beautiful coastline, protected harbors, and variable weather patterns, the Isle of Man provides a playground for water sports aficionados of all abilities. The island has something for everyone, whether you're an expert surfer looking for adrenaline-pumping waves, a leisurely swimmer looking for soothing dips, or a seasoned sailor navigating the wide waters.

Surfing Adventures: Riding the Waves

Surfers will find both tough and rewarding waves around the craggy coastline of the Isle of Man. Popular locations include:

The Point, Port St. Mary: This place is popular among skilled surfers due to its powerful right-hand braking and steady swell.

The cove at Port Erin: This secluded cove has calmer waves that are perfect for novices and longboarders.

Peel's The Chasms: This region boasts a range of breakers for different ability levels, with the "Boiler" providing an exciting challenge for expert surfers.

Beaches & Bays for Swimming in Paradise
The Isle of Man has several beautiful beaches and bays for swimming. Here are a few examples:

Laxey Beach: With calm waves and golden beaches, this gorgeous beach is great for families and leisurely swims.

Port Erin Beach: With beautiful waters and calm waves, this secluded cove is ideal for swimmers of all ages.

Ramsey Beach: Popular among expert swimmers and bodyboarders, this large beach features strong currents.

Port Grenaugh: This quiet cove provides a peaceful retreat with crystal-clear seas and breathtaking coastline views.

Island hopping and coastal cruising on the high seas
Sailing enthusiasts may go on fascinating cruises throughout the Isle of Man, discovering its secret bays and lovely settlements. Consider visiting the Calf of Man, a nature refuge and historic bird sanctuary, for a one-of-a-kind adventure. Popular sailing

destinations include:

Douglas Harbour: The principal harbor on the island allows easy access to the open waters and a range of sailing options.

Peel Harbour: This lovely harbor has a lively ambiance and safe waters for sailing instruction and rentals.

Ramsey Harbour: This ancient port provides stunning views of the island's coastline and acts as a gateway to the island's northern borders.

Additional Activities Beyond the Waves

Beyond surfing, swimming, and sailing, the Isle of Man provides several other water sports experiences. These are some examples:

Stand-up paddleboarding allows you to explore the shoreline at your leisure while taking in the beautiful sights from a new viewpoint.

Kayaking: Discover the island's isolated beaches and wildlife by paddling through secret coves.

Jet skiing allows you to experience the excitement of rushing over the water while feeling the adrenaline rush.

Coasteering: Hike, climb, and swim along the cliffs while admiring the beauty and pushing your physical limitations.

Precautions and safety measures:

When participating in water activities, always put safety first. Keep an eye on the weather and tides, and swim only at authorized beaches with lifeguard supervision. Choose activities that are appropriate for your skill level and experience, and if required, consider taking classes or hiring a guide.

Environmental Awareness:

One of the Isle of Man's greatest treasures is its natural beauty.

Leave no trace, avoid upsetting wildlife, and use sustainable ways to respect the environment.

A Paradise for Water Sports Awaits:

The Isle of Man is a water sports enthusiast's paradise, with different activities for all ability levels. The island provides something for everyone, whether you want an adrenaline thrill on the waves, a refreshing plunge in the water, or a calm cruise around the shoreline. So gather your equipment, enjoy the excitement, and go off on an exciting water sports experience on the Isle of Man.

5

Unveiling the Isle of Man's Rich Heritage: A Cultural and Traditional Journey

The Isle of Man, located in the Irish Sea, has a rich tapestry of centuries of cultural tradition. From ancient Celtic origins to Viking and Norman influences, the island's character is inter-twined with its customs, language, and dynamic community. Immerse yourself in this cultural trip to learn about the Isle of Man's heart and spirit.

Exploring Historical Landmarks: Echoes of the Past

The history of the island may be heard via its old castles and fortified remains. Go back in time to:

   Castle Rushen: A 12th-century fortification overlooking Castletown Bay, with magnificent walls, towers, and rooms that provide an insight into medieval life.

Peel Castle, perched on a rocky islet, functioned as a Viking stronghold and offers stunning panoramic views.

Rushen Abbey: A tranquil 12th-century Cistercian abbey that provides insight into the lives of medieval monks.

Manx National Heritage Sites: Visit ancient sites such as Balladoole Broogh, a fortified Iron Age village, and the Meayll Circle, a mysterious Bronze Age stone circle.

Discovering Manx Gaelic, a Living Language

The Manx Gaelic language, albeit no longer commonly used, has a distinct position in the island's cultural identity. You may hear its distinct noises at:

Manx Language Centre: Located in Douglas, this institution promotes the resurgence of Manx Gaelic via language classes, workshops, and cultural events.

Yn Chruinnaght: Attend the annual Manx Gaelic festival, which includes music, dancing, storytelling, and traditional crafts that celebrate the language and culture.

Manx Gaelic Placenames: Learn about the island's rich history through its place names, many of which are derived from Manx Gaelic and provide historical clues.

3. Festivals and Celebrations: A Tapestry of Traditions

The Isle of Man celebrates its past with lively festivals and customs. Witness the celebrations firsthand:

Hop-tu-Naa: A traditional Halloween ceremony in which youngsters dress up in costumes, sing carols, and get candy.

Tynwald Day: This yearly celebration, held on July 5th, recalls the island's old parliament and includes a colorful parade and ceremony.

The Isle of Man Festival of Motorcycling, often known as the TT, attracts international interest and combines adrenaline-pumping sport with local customs.

Christmas on the Isle of Man: Celebrate the season with traditional songs, adorned towns, and one-of-a-kind Christmas markets.

A Feast for the Senses: A Taste of Manx Cuisine

The culinary culture of the Isle of Man reflects its particular background, presenting a delectable combination of tradition and innovation. Local favorites to try:

Queenies: A Manx delicacy, these petite, sweet scallops are generally served grilled or in a creamy sauce.

Kippers: Smoked herring, a Manx staple eaten for breakfast or as a snack.

Loghtan Lamb: The flesh from this unique breed of sheep is soft and tasty, and it is frequently used in stews, roasts, and pies.

Manx Spiced Meat: A slow-cooked delicacy comprised of meat, spices, and Manx beer that provides a distinct and savory experience.

Manx Cheese: Sample locally manufactured cheeses such as Manx cheddar, smoked cheese, and blue cheese, each with its distinct flavor.

Exploring Local Markets and Galleries in Honor of Craftsmanship

The Isle of Man is home to skilled artisans who preserve old skills. Visit their website to learn more about their work:

Douglas Market: Stalls offering locally manufactured items including knitwear, jewelry, ceramics, and Manx art may be found here.

Guild Galleries: Visit art galleries that feature the work of local artists in a variety of styles and materials.

Cregneash Village: Visit this open-air museum to see traditional Manx crafts and architecture.

Isle of Man Crafts Council: Learn about local craftsmen, courses, and events to immerse yourself in Manx customs.

Discovering Hidden Treasures Of the Beaten Path

Discover the hidden riches of the Isle of Man by venturing beyond the famous tourist destinations:

Manx Species Trust Reserves: Visit the Curraghs Wildlife Park and the Calf of Man to explore the island's different landscapes and view its distinctive species.

Hike through this gorgeous valley with waterfalls, forests, and historic monuments for a calm getaway in nature.

Manx Heritage Railways: Travel back in time on steam trains or horse-drawn trams, learning about the island's transportation history.

Unveiling Manx Culture's Enchanting Tapestry: Traditions, Language, and Music

The Isle of Man, a gem in the Irish Sea, has a distinct and compelling culture, built from old customs, a distinct language, and beautiful melodies of its music. Dive deeper into Manx culture and uncover the soul of this extraordinary island.

A Trip Through Time: Revealing Manx Traditions

Traditions dating back centuries are strongly established in Manx culture, providing insight into the island's rich past and distinct character. Immerse yourself in the following activities:

Yn Chruinnaght: Held in July, this yearly festival celebrates Manx culture via music, dancing, storytelling, and traditional crafts. Witness dynamic Manx dance, listen to the lovely sounds of the bodhrán and clarsach, and feast on local specialties. Participate in courses that teach traditional crafts like wool spinning, knot tying, and weaving, and buy handcrafted souvenirs as a physical remembrance of your cultural immersion.

Hop-tu-Naa: On October 31st, this pre-Christian practice involves youngsters dressing up in costumes and singing songs in return for goodies. Witness the eerie atmosphere and unusual rituals of this ancient Manx event. Visit Cregneash Village, an open-air museum displaying traditional Manx life, and see Hop-tu-Naa rituals like as the burning of the Claasagh, a bonfire said to ward off evil spirits.

Tynwald Day: On July 5th, see the ancient Tynwald ceremonial, which exemplifies the island's long-standing legislative traditions. Watch the colorful parade of government officials and dignitaries dressed in traditional garb, listen to the reading of statutes in English and Manx Gaelic, and take in the joyful mood surrounding this historic occasion.

Explore ancient burial mounds like Cashtal yn Ard and Ballaugh Curragh, standing stones like the Ballaquark Stone Circle, and walled villages like Peel Castle at Manx National Heritage Sites. These locations show the island's interesting history and provide a link to the life of Manx people from centuries ago. Through interactive exhibits and educational displays, visitors may learn about the island's Celtic heritage, Viking influences, and medieval life.

Discovering the Manx Gaelic Language, the Soul of Manx Culture

The Manx Gaelic language, which was formerly the main language of the Isle of Man, is undergoing a comeback. Embrace the beauty and significance of this language by:

Manx Language Centre: Located in Douglas, this center promotes the Manx Gaelic language by offering language classes, workshops, and events. Learn fundamental words, comprehend the language's distinctive syntax and structure, and help its continuing rebirth. Participate in language exchange programs and discussion groups to obtain practical experience speaking Manx Gaelic with native speakers.

Manx Gaelic Placenames: Learn about Manx culture by exploring the island's geography and deciphering place names. Discover how these names, which are frequently Gaelic in origin, reflect the island's history, geography, and mythology. Discover the history behind evocative names like Cronk ny Arrey Laa (Hill of the Day of the Slaughter) and Ballaugh (Dwelling Place of the Kings).

Listen to traditional Manx music, which frequently includes songs and lyrics in Manx Gaelic. The beautiful melodies and lyrical words provide a rare glimpse into Manx culture and its strong connection to the land and its people. Support local musicians by purchasing records and attending Manx Gaelic music events.

Yn Cheshaght Ghailckagh: This non-profit promotes the Manx Gaelic language and culture. To discover more about the language and its significance to the Isle of Man, visit their website or attend one of their events. Volunteer for various activities, such as language lessons for children and adults, and help to resuscitate this unique language.

Manx Music's Haunting Melodies:

Manx music captures the island's history, traditions, and emotions via fascinating melodies and complex narratives. Investigate the thriving musical scene:

Traditional Music Sessions: Attend vibrant sessions at pubs such as "The Bay" in Port Erin and cultural centers such as the Peel Centenary Centre. Listen to the bodhrán, violin, and clarsach weave their spell, evoking a sense of shared delight and cultural connection. Participate in the dancing and singing to feel the contagious spirit of Manx music for yourself.

Festivals: Attend festivals such as Yn Chruinnaght, the Isle of Man Festival of Music and Dance, and the Peel Music Festival to experience the varied spectrum of Manx music, which includes everything from old folk tunes to modern works. Enjoy

Unveiling Historical Sites on the Isle of Man

. As we travel through time, we'll visit the island's fascinating historical landmarks, each of which tells a different story about Manx's heritage.

The hauntingly magnificent Peel Castle, which stands majestically on St. Patrick's Isle, is our first destination on this historical voyage. This medieval masterpiece may be found in the coordinates 54.2249° N and 4.6980° W. The stone walls of the castle, formerly a bastion of Viking warriors, reverberate tales of wars, bishops, and the sea's rhythmic lullaby. Peel Castle is located on the Isle of Man, tucked away in the Irish Sea, and has a rich tapestry of history just waiting to be discovered Peel, Isle of Man.

Moving east, we come upon Castle Rushen, a living testimony to the Isle's medieval heritage. This castle, located at 54.2279° N, 4.6907° W, has watched centuries unfold inside its strong grasp. Immerse yourself in the medieval great hall's atmosphere and discover the complex tunnels that preserve the mysteries of a bygone period. Castle Rushen is located in Castletown, Isle of Man.

Our historical journey takes us to Castletown's Nautical Museum, a treasure mine for nautical fans. This museum, located at 54.0751° N, 4.6509° W, traces the island's nautical history and honors its naval heroes. Explore elaborately built ship models and relics that tell the stories of courageous sailors who sailed the Irish Sea. The Nautical Museum is located in The Quay in Castletown, Isle of Man.

Manx Heritage: Museum Openings

Dive into the heart of Douglas, where the Manx Museum welcomes you. This cultural hub, located at 54.1501° N and 4.4850° W, embodies the Isle's history and legacy. Each exhibit unfolds like a compelling novel, from the island's Celtic beginnings to the Viking assaults. Manx Museum is located in Kingswood Grove in Douglas, Isle of Man.

In Laxey, explore the Laxey Wheel and Mines Trail, a living memorial to the island's industrial past. This landmark, located at 54.2360° N, 4.3948° W, celebrates the Victorian innovation that fueled the Isle's mining economy. Discover the stories of the miners who worked under the earth's surface, altering the economic landscape of the island. Laxey Wheel and Mines Trail is located on Mines Road in Laxey, Isle of Man.

Manx History: Revealing Majestic Castles

Our voyage concludes in the picturesque environs of Balladoole, where the Balladoole Viking Burial Site sits solemnly at 54.0641° N, 4.6999° W. This burial cemetery, which is both peaceful and strong, speaks of Viking chieftains who once dominated these territories. The tranquil scenery conceals the warrior spirits who sleep underneath, providing insight into the island's Norse origins. Balladoole Viking Burial Site is located in Balladoole, Isle of Man.

As we come to the end of our journey through Manx heritage, these historical buildings, museums, and grand castles serve as reminders of the Isle of Man's rich and varied history. Allow the echoes of ages past to guide you through the small hallways of magnificent stone edifices, beckoning you to unearth the stories inscribed into the very fabric of this enthralling island. May your path be as timeless as the history around you.

Culinary Delights: From Kippers to Queenies, Savoring Manx Cuisine

Explore the Isle of Man's gourmet offerings, where traditional flavors blend harmoniously with the island's natural richness. Manx food is a tapestry of flavors waiting to be discovered, with everything from smokey kippers to delicious queenies.

Our gastronomic adventure begins at the tiny community of Port St. Mary, which is famed for its scenic coastline and a culinary jewel known as The Fish House, which is located at 54.0833° N, 4.7072° W. This seaside restaurant creates a gourmet symphony with locally produced fish, a characteristic of Manx gastronomy. The Fish House is located on Bay View Road in Port St. Mary, Isle of Man.

Explore the secrets of Manx kippers at Moore's Traditional Curers, located at 54.2251° N, 4.6954° W in the heart of Peel. For almost a century, the delicate skill of smoking herring has been developed here, imparting these preserved jewels with a particular taste that captivates the palette. Moore's Traditional Curers is located in East Quay in Peel, Isle of Man.

As we go inland, the hamlet of Laxey, located at 54.2391° N, 4.3935° W, beckons with a gastronomic treasure trove—La Mona Lisa. This lovely café combines traditional Manx foods with continental flare, resulting in a menu that honors both local traditions and global influences. La Mona Lisa is located on Glen Road in Laxey, Isle of Man.

Continuing on our journey, we arrive at the Tynwald Hill Inn in St. John's, which is conveniently located at 54.2392° N, 4.5505° W. This old inn, set among rolling hills, provides substantial Manx delicacies like the legendary Queenie Scallops, demonstrating the island's dedication to maintaining culinary traditions. Tynwald Hill Inn is located on Main Road in St. John's, Isle of Man.

In the heart of Castletown, at 54.0768° N, 4.6503° W, the Ballamenagh Café invites you to experience handcrafted pleasures in a comfortable ambiance. From exquisite cakes to savory pies, this institution embodies Manx's friendliness. Ballamenagh Café is located at 10 Arbory Street in Castletown, Isle of Man.

Our gastronomic journey comes to an end in The Cat with No Tail, a busy pub at 54.1534° N, 4.4809° W in Douglas. Traditional Manx cooking meets a lively ambiance here, making it the ideal place to unwind after a day of exploring. The Cat with No Tail is located on the Promenade in Douglas, Isle of Man.

With its emphasis on fresh, local products and time-honored recipes, Manx cuisine provides a one-of-a-kind and remarkable gastronomic experience. Each taste is a celebration of the Isle of Man's unique culinary heritage, from the salty embrace of kippers to the delicate sweetness of queenies. May you discover the genuine spirit of Manx hospitality as you delight in these tastes, where every meal tells a narrative and leaves you wanting more.

Festivals & Events: Celebrating the Vibrant Cultural Mosaic of the Isle of Man

Welcome to the Isle of Man, where a festive atmosphere

pervades the air and cultural events spread like bright tapestries, weaving together traditions, music, and communal friendliness. Join us as we explore the island's unique cultural mosaic through a broad assortment of festivals and activities.

The Isle of Man Film Festival kicks off our tour in the heart of Douglas, the Isle of Man's city. This cinematic event, located at 54.1501° N, 4.4850° W, attracts both film aficionados and industry experts. The festival not only shows foreign films but also local talent, cultivating a strong respect for the craft of storytelling via the lens. The Isle of Man Film Festival is held at the Broadway Cinema, Villa Marina, Harris Promenade, Douglas, Isle of Man.

Moving east, the lovely town of Laxey holds the Fair Day of the Laxey and Lonan Heritage Trust. This festival, located at 54.2360° N, 4.3948° W, is a nostalgic excursion into the island's past, complete with traditional games, live music, and handcrafted products. It offers an enthralling peek into the Isle's rich cultural legacy while fostering a spirit of pleasure and togetherness. Laxey and Lonan Heritage Trust, Glen Road, Laxey, Isle of Man.

As we travel south, the southern village of Castletown greets us with the Rushen Abbey Open Day. This event, located at 54.0737° N, 4.6520° W, brings to life the remains of a medieval monastery. The open day includes historical reenactments and guided excursions that highlight the island's profound connection to its past. Rushen Abbey Open Day is held at Ballasalla, Isle of Man.

Continue your trip to Peel, where the Peel Traditional Boat Weekend takes place along the scenic shoreline at 54.2249° N, 4.6980° W. With historic boat displays, sea shanties, and maritime-themed activities that generate a sense of nostalgia and pride, this nautical festival pays respect to the Isle's seafaring past. Peel Traditional Boat Weekend is located in Peel, Isle of Man.

Our tour across the Isle of Man's cultural calendar takes us to the Yn Chruinnaght Celtic Gathering, a celebration of Celtic music, dancing, and culture located at 54.1501° N, 4.4850° W in Douglas. This worldwide festival is a melting pot of Celtic traditions, bringing together artists and audiences in a joyful celebration of shared history. Yn Chruinnaght Celtic Gathering is located in Villa Marina, Harris Promenade, Douglas, Isle of Man.

The spectacle of the Isle of Man TT Races, an internationally famous event that captivates adrenaline junkies worldwide, brings our exploration to a close. The TT Races, held at 54.1501° N, 4.4850° W, bring together motorcyclists, spectators, and thrill-seekers for a fortnight of speed, skill, and unprecedented excitement. Address: Isle of Man TT Races, several places across the island.

As we reflect on the festivals and events that fill the Isle of Man's cultural calendar, we can't help but be impressed by the island's diversity and energy. From the Film Festival's creative energy to the Traditional Boat Weekend's rhythmic pulses, each event adds a distinct brushstroke to the canvas of the Isle's cultural diversity. Participate in the celebrations, embrace the customs, and become a part of the enduring stories that unfold in this enchanting corner of the world.

6

Additional Resources: Plan Your Isle of Man Trip Confidently

The Isle of Man travel is a thrilling adventure, and having access to vital information is critical to ensuring a smooth experience. These additional resources can help you plan your Isle of Man journey with confidence, from studying the island's weather patterns to locating hidden treasures off the usual road.

Understanding the Weather on the Isle of Man: Navigating the Seasons

The climate of the Isle of Man is a kaleidoscope of ever-changing weather, and recognizing its intricacies is critical for planning a pleasurable trip. The island, located in the Irish Sea at 54.2361° N, 4.5481° W, has a moderate marine climate. The Isle of Man is the address.

Summer (June to August): This is the busiest season for tourists, with longer days and warmer temperatures ranging from 14°C to 18°C (57°F to 64°F). It's the perfect season for outdoor activities, exploring coastal paths, and taking in the vivid ambiance of the island. Pack layers, sunscreen, and a waterproof jacket in case of rain.

fall (September to November): As fall approaches, the land-scape takes on golden hues. Temperatures vary from 10°C and 14°C (50°F and 57°F). It's an excellent time to go trekking and appreciate the changing environment. Prepare for cooler evenings and the possibility of rain, and don't forget to bring a strong pair of walking shoes.

Winter (December to February): Shorter days and lower tem-peratures range from 2°C to 8°C (36°F to 46°F). While snowfall is uncommon, the Isle radiates a tranquil appeal. Warm layers, waterproof apparel, and sturdy boots are required, especially when venturing into the harsh interior.

Spring (March to May): See the island come alive with blooming flowers and longer days. Temperatures in the spring range from 5°C to 10°C (41°F to 50°F). It's a great time for seaside walks and learning about the island's unique fauna. Pack layers and rainproof gear for unpredictable weather.

Consult the Isle of Man Weather Service for real-time weather updates during your travel. 54.2361° N, 4.5481° W are the coordinates. The Isle of Man Weather Service is located at Ronaldsway Airport in Ballasalla, Isle of Man. This tool delivers reliable and up-to-date forecasts, allowing you to organize your daily activities around the weather.

Island Exploration: Hidden Treasures Beyond the Main Attrac-

tions

While famous monuments and popular sites lure visitors, the genuine soul of the Isle of Man may be found in its hidden jewels, which await the observant traveler. Navigate your tour with the following insights on the island's lesser-known treasures.

Balladoole Viking Ship Burial: Learn about the island's Viking origins at the Balladoole Viking Ship Burial, which is located near Castletown. 54.0621° N, 4.6609° W are the coordinates. Balladoole Viking Ship Burial is located on Balladoole Road in Castletown, Isle of Man. This archeological site exposes the burial of a Viking ship and gives insight into the island's complex past.

Cregneash Folk Village: At Cregneash Folk Village, you may immerse yourself in the island's agrarian history. 54.0732° N, 4.7744° W are the coordinates. Cregneash Folk Village is located in Cregneash, Isle of Man. This living museum depicts traditional Manx village life, complete with thatched huts, farm animals, and costumed guides who provide information about the island's cultural past.

The Chasms: Discover geological wonders at The Chasms, which is located at 54.1080° N, 4.6829° W. Derbyhaven, Isle of Man (The Chasms). These breathtaking coastline formations, which resemble deep gashes in the rocks, create a captivating setting. The location provides a one-of-a-kind chance for seaside hikes and photography.

Sulby Claddagh: Explore the serene beauty of Sulby Claddagh, which is located at 54.3428° N, 4.4744° W. Sulby Claddagh is located in Sulby, Isle of Man. This gorgeous nature reserve offers a tranquil lake surrounded by thick flora, making it ideal for a relaxing vacation and superb birding.

Port Erin Railway Museum: The Port Erin Railway Museum delves into the island's railway history. 54.0920° N, 4.7615° W are the coordinates. Port Erin Railway Museum is located on Station Road in Port Erin, Isle of Man. The museum, housed in a disused railway station, displays historic locomotives, carriages, and artifacts from the Isle of Man Railway's illustrious past.

Transportation Hints: Easily Navigate the Isle

Exploring the different landscapes of the Isle of Man requires efficient transportation. Whether you prefer the romanticism of vintage trains or the ease of modern buses, these transportation recommendations will ensure pleasant and pleasurable travel.

The Manx Electric Railway: Take a nostalgic ride down the island's eastern shore on the Manx Electric Railway. 54.1501° N, 4.4809° W are the coordinates. The Manx Electric Railway is located at Derby Castle in Douglas, Isle of Man. This old electric tramway runs from Douglas to Ramsey, providing stunning views and a sense of nostalgia.

Isle of Man Bus Services:* Use the Isle of Man Bus Services to go about the island's towns and villages.

Man Bus Services. Coordinates: Various bus stations are located across the island. These extensive services link important places, allowing you to comfortably explore the Isle's different areas. Examine the timetable for convenient travel times.

Steam Railway Adventure: Board the Isle of Man Steam Railway for a steam-powered excursion. 54.2324° N, 4.3930° W are the coordinates. The Isle of Man Steam Railway is located in Douglas, Isle of Man. This old railway runs through the lush scenery of the island, giving a picturesque route from Douglas to Port Erin. Relax and take in the beautiful scenery.

Car Rentals: Car rentals are available at sites such as Ronaldsway Airport for individuals seeking flexibility. 54.0841° N, 4.6343° W are the coordinates. Ronaldsway Airport is located in Ballasalla, Isle of Man. Renting a car allows you to see off-the-beaten-path locations and adjust your schedule to your specific needs.

Isle of Man Airport Transfers: Reliable airport transfer services ensure a seamless arrival and departure experience. 54.0841° N, 4.6343° W are the coordinates. Isle of Man Airport is located at Ballasalla, Isle of Man. Several taxi and shuttle services are available, making it easy to get to and from your hotel.

Accommodation: Creating a Home Away from Home

Choosing the correct hotel for your trip to the Isle of Man is critical. Whether you prefer the beauty of a boutique hotel or the peace of a countryside bed & breakfast, the island has a variety of accommodations to suit every traveler's preferences.

The Claremont Hotel: The Claremont Hotel in Douglas immerses you in luxury. 54.1529° N, 4.4885° W are the coordinates. The Claremont Hotel is located at 18-22 Loch Promenade in Douglas, Isle of Man. This magnificent hotel overlooks the bay and combines modern luxury with Victorian charm. Enjoy large apartments, superb restaurants, and stunning views of the sea.

Glen Helen Inn: Enjoy the peace of the countryside at Glen Helen Inn. 54.2366° N, 4.5887° W are the coordinates. Glen Helen Inn is located in Glen Helen, Isle of Man. This inn, located in the lovely Glen Helen, provides pleasant accommodations, a warm ambiance, and proximity to scenic walking paths.

Cronk Darragh Cottage: At Cronk Darragh Cottage, you may experience the elegance of a self-catering cottage. 54.2258° N, 4.4703° W are the coordinates. Cronk Darragh Cottage is located in Peel, Isle of Man. This ancient Manx cottage offers a pleasant and personal location in which to explore the island at your leisure.

The Empress Hotel: From The Empress Hotel, you can explore the ancient town of Douglas. 54.1505° N, 4.4782° W are the coordinates. The Empress Hotel is located on the Central Promenade in Douglas, Isle of Man. This renowned hotel combines Victorian grandeur with modern comforts, giving it an ideal starting point for your urban travels.

Knockaloe Beg Farm: At Knockaloe Beg Farm, you may immerse yourself in rural peace. 54.3228° N, 4.5478° W are the coordinates. Knockaloe Beg Farm is located in Patrick, Isle of Man. This functioning farm provides self-catering cottages, allowing you to experience farm life while staying in comfortable accommodations.

Savoring Manx Flavors: Local Cuisine and Dining

Exploring the Isle of Man includes a culinary trip, where local tastes and traditional dishes highlight the island's rich gastronomic past. Indulge your appetite in the numerous gastronomic selections, which range from hearty pub grub to fine seafood.

The Creek Inn, Peel: Begin your gastronomic excursion in Peel with The Creek Inn. 54.2345° N, 4.6399° W are the coordinates. The Creek Inn is located at Old Laxey Hill in Peel, Isle of Man. This historic tavern emphasizes the island's maritime charm, with a cuisine that features freshly caught fish and local products.

The Tea Junction, Douglas: Enjoy an afternoon tea at The Tea Junction in Douglas. 54.1497° N, 4.4797° W are the coordinates. The Tea Junction is located at 29-31 North Quay in Douglas, Isle of Man. With its antique ambiance, this quaint tearoom provides an assortment of teas, sandwiches, and scrumptious pastries, giving a comfortable respite in the center of the capital.

The Abbey, Ballasalla: The Abbey in Ballasalla serves modern Manx cuisine. 54.0823° N, 4.6304° W are the coordinates. The Abbey is located at Malew Street in Ballasalla, Isle of Man. This gastropub mixes regional cuisine with foreign influences, providing a broad menu and a warm atmosphere.

Little Fish Café, Douglas: Indulge in fish delicacies at Douglas' Little Fish Café. 54.1515° N, 4.4816° W are the coordinates. Little Fish Café is located at 59 Duke Street in Douglas, Isle of Man. This tiny restaurant honors the island's maritime riches by presenting meals made from locally sourced fish and shellfish.

The Sound Café, Cregneash: Culminate your gastronomic discovery at Cregneash's The Sound Café. 54.0615° N, 4.8262°

W are the coordinates. The Sound Café is located on Sound Road in Cregneash, Isle of Man. This café, which overlooks the Calf of Man, serves a cuisine that highlights Manx products, giving a great balance of flavors and breathtaking vistas.

Festivals & Events: Celebrating the Vibrant Culture of the Isle of Man**

Participate in the Isle of Man's colorful festivals and events and immerse yourself in its cultural tapestry. These events, which range from exciting music festivals to historical reen-actments, provide a unique view into the island's dynamic background.

Isle of Man TT Races: Get your adrenaline pumping with the Isle of Man TT Races. Coordinates: Several places on the island. This legendary motorcycle racing event, held each year in late May and early June, attracts fans from all around the world. Feel the rush as racers face the island's difficult roadways.

Manx Music Festival: The Manx Music Festival, often known as the Guild, showcases the island's musical ability. Coordinates: Various Douglas locations. This week-long event, held in April, features a wide spectrum of acts.

The Official Isle of Man Tourism Website: Your All-In-One Guide*

As you begin to plan your Isle of Man vacation, the Official Isle of Man Tourism Website serves as your virtual portal to a wealth of information. The Isle of Man, located amid the Irish Sea at 54.2361° N, 4.5481° W, is a sanctuary for adventurers seeking diverse landscapes, rich history, and dynamic culture. The Isle of Man is the address.

How to Unlock the Portal:

Go to the official website at [isleofman.com]. com](https://www.isleofman.com/) to gain access to a plethora of information that can help shape your trip. Immerse yourself in the user-friendly interface intended to meet the demands of every traveler. The site mixes practicality and aesthetics in a way that reflects the Isle's dedication to offering a great user experience.

Explore the Isle:

Begin your adventure by exploring the 'Discover' area, which highlights the Isle's distinctive attractions. The iconic Laxey Wheel, the world's largest working waterwheel, is located at coordinates 54.2352° N, 4.3959° W, Address: Laxey Wheel, Mines Road, Laxey, Isle of Man, and the medieval splendor of Castle Rushen in Castletown is located at coordinates 54.0744° N, 4.6517° W, Address: Castle Rushen, Castletown, Isle of Man.

How to Plan Your Stay:

Moving on to the 'Plan Your Stay' area, you'll find a thorough guide to lodgings that will help you make the best option for your needs. The website gives thorough listings, whether you are looking for the seaside appeal of Peel or the tranquillity of the countryside in Sulby. Peel, for example, has the coordinates 54.2249° N, 4.6980° W, and the address Peel, Isle of Man.

Calendar of Events:

The 'activities' area reveals the dynamic calendar of the Isle, ensuring you don't miss cultural festivals, athletic activities, or community meetings. The coordinates for the annual Isle of Man TT Races vary since they take place all across the island. Keep up to speed on exciting races and celebrations that will add a dynamic aspect to your vacation.

Interactive Maps:

Interactive maps are a navigational benefit for the adventurer at heart. The maps give a virtual compass for your travel, whether you're charting the shoreline along the A2 road, coordinates 54.1535° N, 4.4806° W, Address: Douglas to Castletown, Isle of Man, or arranging a pleasant drive through the magnificent landscapes.

Useful Information:

Explore the 'Practical Information' area to learn about anything from transportation to emergency services. Understand the local customs, like as the respectful greeting of "Hello" or "Moghrey mie," and empower yourself with the information that will enable smooth contact with the welcoming Manx population.

Getting in Touch with Nature:

The natural beauty of the Isle of Man is highlighted in the 'Nature and Wildlife' section, which reveals different ecosystems ranging from coastal reserves to woodland glens. Sulby Claddagh is located at 54.3428° N, 4.4744° W, and the address is Sulby Claddagh, Sulby, Isle of Man. Explore the wildlife of the island and organize encounters with seals, seagulls, and the elusive wallabies in the south.

Your Culinary Adventure:

The 'Food and Drink' section reveals the Isle's culinary riches to foodies. The Creek Inn is located at 54.2345° N, 4.6399° W, and the location is The Creek Inn, Old Laxey Hill, Peel, Isle of Man. From kippers to Queenies, the gastronomic options on the Isle are a feast for the senses.

Remain Informed:

The 'News and Offers' area keeps you up to speed on travel warnings, weather updates, and current happenings. This guarantees that your travel is not only entertaining but also up to-date with the most recent information.

How to Plan Your Wedding:

The 'Weddings' area is a treasure mine of inspiration and practical assistance for people considering the Isle of Man as a wedding destination. The picturesque vistas of the Isle provide a stunning background for an unforgettable celebration.

Inclusion and accessibility:

Accessibility and inclusion sections highlight the Isle's dedication to welcoming all guests. Discover wheelchair-accessible attractions, accessible lodging, and the warm embrace of a welcoming community.

The Official Isle of Man Tourism Website is more than just a guide; it is your digital companion, providing a deep insight into the island's character. From arranging your travel to immersing yourself in the Isle's cultural tapestry, the website is a valuable ally in ensuring that your stay is more than simply a holiday but an amazing expedition.

Isle of Man Travel Blog: Insider Information on Local Experiences

While the official website gives a thorough overview, the Isle of Man Travel Blog provides a more intimate and personal viewpoint, exposing the island's hidden jewels and local experiences. Explore the world through the eyes of seasoned travelers and locals alike, obtaining insights that go beyond traditional guidebooks.

How to Use the Blog:
Explore the Isle of Man Travel Blog at [isleofmantravel-blog.com]. com](https://www.isleofmantravelblog.com/) to delve into the tales, anecdotes, and firsthand experiences that bring the island's stories to life. With its visually appealing style, the blog acts as a digital tapestry of experiences, allowing you to go on virtual travels.

Local Adventures:
Local contributors share their adventures, bringing you off the beaten road to uncover the spirit of the Isle. Whether it's an unusual walk along the Raad ny Foillan seaside walkway, coordinates 54.2177° N, 4.4802° W, Address: Raad ny Foillan,

Isle of Man, or a meeting with the elusive Manx wallabies, each article reveals a different side of the island.

Kitchen Chronicles:

Explore the culinary treasures of the Isle via culinary chronicles that go beyond the table. The site immerses you in the gastronomic tapestry of the island, from foraging trips for wild garlic in Glen Maye to the craftsmanship of producing the perfect Manx Bonnag.

Photography Essays:

Storytelling via images

Photographic essays portraying the natural beauty of the Isle take center stage. Explore photographs of foggy vistas in Snaefell, 54.2586° N, 4.4245° W, Address: Snaefell, Isle of Man, or the architectural beauty of small communities like Port St. Mary.

Hideaway Spots:

Discover secret havens and quiet areas that exemplify the Isle's tranquillity. Groudle Glen's coordinates are 54.2748° N, 4.4542° W, and its address is Groudle Glen, Onchan, Isle of Man. The site reveals sanctuaries where time appears to stand still, whether it's a tucked-away tearoom or a sun-kissed cove.

The Chronicles of the Community:

Explore the dynamic community life by reading chronicles of local festivals, events, and traditions. Explore the contagious energy of the annual Castletown Ale Festival, 54.0743° N, 4.6499° W, Address: Castletown Ale Festival, Castletown, Isle of Man, or the camaraderie of traditional Manx dance.

Adventure Journals:

Explore the blog's adventure diaries, where contributors discuss their experiences ascending the steep slopes of Bradda Head, coordinates 54.0728° N, 4.7658° W, Address: Bradda Head, Port Erin, Isle of Man, or cycling along Glen Mooar's gorgeous pathways.

Local Artists and Craftspeople:

Meet local artisans and craftspeople via features that dive into the Isle's creative pulse. The coordinates for a prominent Manx potter's workshop are 54.3082° N, 4.4698° W, and the address is Isle of Man Pottery, Ramsey, Isle of Man. Discover ancient crafts and the tales that are woven into each masterpiece.

Seasonal Amusements:

The blog captures the atmosphere of seasonal celebrations, from the mystical allure of Christmas markets in Douglas to the exuberance of the annual Tynwald Day celebrations. Tynwald Hill's coordinates are 54.2315° N, 4.5466° W, and its address is Tynwald Hill, St John's, Isle of Man. Immerse yourself in the celebrations that accompany each season.

Local Perspectives:

The Isle of Man Travel Blog is a chorus of local voices, not just a collection of stories. Contributors express their love of the Isle, creating an original and diverse story that mirrors the different experiences available on this wonderful island.

Practical Insider Advice:

In addition to the compelling storytelling, the blog provides practical insider insights, ensuring that your journey is not only full of wonder but also smoothly matched with the rhythm of local life. From the finest times to see ancient ruins to the greatest places to catch a sunrise, the blog is a wealth of knowledge.

You're not simply absorbing information when you browse the Isle of Man Travel Blog; you're starting on an adventure with other explorers. It's an invitation to see the Isle through the eyes of people who have been enchanted by its appeal, providing a personalized and enlightening viewpoint that goes beyond traditional tourist guides.

Connecting with the Isle of Man Community on Social Media

As you plan your trip to the Isle of Man, keep in mind that the modern traveler's toolset now includes more than just guidebooks and maps. Social media has become your digital compass in the era of connection, weaving a tapestry of real-time experiences and community insights. Join the virtual adventure as we investigate methods to interact with the Isle of Man community via social media.

Isle of Man coordinates:
- N 54.2361° Latitude
- Latitude: 4.5481° West

Facebook: Isle Explorers' Community Hub
On the Isle of Man, Facebook, the historic town square of the digital age, pulsates with life. It's a vibrant environment

to become familiar with the local mood, with everything from community forums to event sites.

Pages for Communities:

Go to the Facebook page for the Isle of Man Community. Travelers and locals congregate here, exchanging advice and tales and answering questions. Members exchange anecdotes about hidden jewels, local events, and the greatest sites for panoramic sunsets, and the sense of community is evident.

Awesome Events:

Use Facebook's Events section to plan your vacation around the Isle's pulse. Whether it's the yearly Isle of Man TT Races, with coordinates fluctuating around the island, or the quaint Port Erin Beer Festival, with coordinates 54.0869° N, 4.7614° W, Address: Port Erin, Isle of Man, Facebook keeps you updated.

Local Companies:

Follow and interact with Isle of Man companies to support local businesses. Your Facebook feed becomes a curated tour of the Isle's offerings, from odd eateries with coordinates like 54.2322° N, 4.3861° W, Address: Noa Bakehouse, 18-Welcome to the Isle of Man, an amazing island set in the Irish Sea with Celtic charm, rugged vistas, and a rich cultural tapestry. Set off on an amazing tour with this thorough book, designed to help you plan your ideal Isle of Man experience.

Uncovering the Treasures of the Isle of Man: Must-See Locations

Peel Castle sits as a powerful sentinel on a rocky islet off the coast of Peel, murmuring tales of Vikings, lords, and sieges. Explore the island's towers, dungeons, and Great Keep, and immerse yourself in its fascinating past.

Laxey Wheel: Behold the engineering marvel that is the world's largest operating waterwheel, the Laxey Wheel. Witness its magnificent rotation, which was formerly used to pump water from Laxey Mines, and travel back in time to the island's industrial history.

Rushen Castle: Rushen Castle, a towering fortress that has kept vigil over the island for generations, transports you to the heart of Manx history. Explore its medieval towers, battlements, and Great Hall to learn about Manx royalty.

Immerse Yourself in Manx Traditions Through Cultural Tapestry

Manx Museum: Explore the rich past of the Isle of Man at the Manx Museum, a treasure trove of relics, exhibitions, and interactive displays. Travel back in time, from ancient settlements to Viking attacks and Victorian traditions, to obtain a better grasp of the island's distinct culture.

Cregneash Folk Village: A living museum that recreates traditional Manx life, Cregneash Folk Village transports visitors back in time. Wander among thatched huts, investigate the blacksmith's forge, and get a personal look at the island's agricultural past.

Manx National Heritage: Immerse yourself in the cultural fabric of the Isle of Man by visiting the Manx National Heritage sites and attractions. Learn about the island's rich history and culture by exploring its ancient burial sites, Viking villages, and medieval castles.

Marina Road, Douglas, Isle of Man, to artisanal boutiques displaying Manx workmanship.

Instagram: Manx Wonders Visual Odyssey

Instagram turns your trip story into a visual voyage, and the Isle of Man's stunning landscapes serve as the ideal canvas.

Unveiling Beauty Hashtags:

Begin your investigation by looking for popular Isle of Man hashtags such as #IOM, #IsleofMan, or #ManxViews. These tags display a mosaic of photos ranging from the craggy cliffs of Maughold, coordinates 54.3742° N, 4.3736° W, Address: Maughold, Isle of Man, to the tranquil serenity of Laxey Wheel.

Local Influencers include:

Follow local influencers that embody the Isle's character. Their carefully selected feeds provide a personalized tour, revealing hidden jewels, gastronomic gems, and the ever-changing moods of the Irish Sea. Port St. Mary's coordinates are 54.0847° N, 4.7074° W, and its address is Port St. Mary, Isle of Man.

Interactive Narratives:

Use Instagram Stories to get a real-time experience. Local companies frequently provide behind-the-scenes views, event highlights, and spontaneous anecdotes that lend a sense of authenticity to your online exploration.

Twitter: Manx Twittersphere Conversations

Twitter, the buzzing marketplace of ideas, presents you with the Isle's dynamic pulse. Follow @visitisleofman and #Isleof-ManHour for a direct connection to the Manx Twittersphere.

Instant Updates:

Twitter excels at providing real-time updates. Follow accounts linked to public transportation, such as @IOMAirport and @iombusandrail, to remain up to date on any changes or recommendations for navigating the island with ease.

Local Perspectives:

Participate in talks about popular Manx issues to connect with local perspectives. Twitter links you with the heartbeat of the Isle, whether it's the island's rich history, outdoor excursions, or the current cultural occurrences.

YouTube: Manx Adventures Come to Life

Through cinematic vlogs, documentaries, and immersive travelogues, YouTube, the visual storyteller, brings you to the Isle of Man.

Locals' Vlogs:

Take virtual trips using vlogs recorded by Manx residents. From a hike up Snaefell, coordinates 54.2550° N, 4.4249° W, Address: Snaefell, Isle of Man, to a coastal car drive along the A2, YouTubers share intimate insights into the diverse activities available on the Isle.

Historical Reveals:

Explore the channels that dive into the rich history of the Isle. Documentaries on historic sites such as Peel Castle coordinates 54.2252° N, 4.6981° W, Address: Peel Castle, Peel, Isle of Man, or haunting legends of the Fairy Bridge enrich your awareness of the island.

Adventures Off the Beaten Path:

YouTube is a portal to excursions off the beaten path. Hike the Raad ny Foillan coastal walk, coordinates 54.2166° N, 4.4802° W, Address: Raad ny Foillan, Isle of Man, or go sea kayaking around the rough coastline with the designers.

LinkedIn Professional Perspectives on Island Opportunities

LinkedIn adds a professional perspective to your discovery of the Isle of Man, connecting you with local companies, employment possibilities, and intelligent discussions.

Local Business Perspectives:

Follow Isle of Man-based businesses on LinkedIn to learn more about the island's dynamic business sector. Engage with local entrepreneurs' posts to gather insights on the economic scene and new trends.

Professional Networking:

Join LinkedIn groups connected to sectors of interest if you're looking for professional possibilities on the Isle. These clubs provide a forum for networking, discussion, and learning about job opportunities.

Seminars and Events:

LinkedIn can keep you up to date on local events, seminars, and workshops. From industry-specific events to skill development courses, we have it all.

These events provide an opportunity to network with professionals on the Isle.

Finally, social media is more than simply a way to share your Isle of Man journey; it's a gateway to a thriving community ready to offer its tales, insights, and warm welcome. When you connect with the Isle via Facebook, Instagram, Twitter, YouTube, and LinkedIn, you become part of a digital caravan traveling both the physical and virtual landscapes of the Isle of Man. Each post, tweet, or video becomes a brushstroke in the ongoing painting that is the Isle's tale.

come a part of the timeless stories that unfold in this magical corner of the globe.